I0222596

SASQUATCH

As a career law enforcement officer, I am by nature a skeptic, but a good mystery is always worth investigating— particularly so if it affords an excuse to spend one's vacations deep in the great forests of the Pacific Northwest or traveling around the country interviewing people with interesting stories. My thirteen years spent investigating Bigfoot has convinced me he exists.

~ the late Ken Coon

Ken Coon

Prepared for publication by

Joe R. Blakely & Pat Edwards

Oregon Authors and Historians

Copyright © 2019
by Joe R. Blakely & Pat Edwards

All rights reserved. No part of the material protected
by this copyright notice may be reproduced or

utilized in any form or by any means,
electronic or

mechanical, including photocopying,

recording or by any informational
storage and retrieval system without written
permission from the copyright owner.

First Edition, 2019

Front & back cover illustration by
M. Salyers Hamilton; 1969
(These illustrations accompanied the manuscript that
Ken Coon wrote in the mid-1970s)

Published by

Groundwaters Publishing, LLC
P.O. Box 50, Lorane, Oregon 97451
http://www.groundwaterspublishing.com

ISBN- 978-0-9964261-4-5

Foreword
by Joe R. Blakely

Since writing my fiction stories about Bigfoot in an ancient forest, there have been some unexplained happenings in my own life. But first, let me explain...

I actually saw Bigfoot on a lonely gravel road in the Coast Range Mountains near Alsea Falls' campground. It happened early one spring morning in1990, while I was headed to plant Douglas fir trees near Waldport, Oregon. My dog, Rosebud, was with me at the time, but I'm not sure whether she saw Bigfoot or not.

Bigfoot lumbered across the road, about 30 yards in front of my red pickup truck. He walked from the forest on my right to the other side of the road. He seemed unaware I was there and blended into the forest on the other side. Before this encounter, I had not thought much about Bigfoot. It happened so fast, was so unexpected, and seemed so ordinary, it hardly roused my curiosity. Had I been more knowledgeable about the creature, I might have gotten out of the truck and tried to find some footprints, mark the exact spot where I'd seen him, or anything that would help confirm my story. I was intent on planting trees, however, so kept on driving.

Since that time, I have read interesting accounts about old growth forests and how vital they are to our planet. So I created the stories about Bigfoot in an 1933 old-growth forest.

Since writing my fiction stories, I have met many people who have told me their stories about Bigfoot. Just recently, a lady scientist told me she was in a Western Canada old-growth forest and found a huge footprint. "Could have only been Bigfoot's," she said. She was dead serious.

A month before that, a man stopped by my table at the Eugene Holiday Market, and said, "Do you want to hear my story about Bigfoot?"

"Sure," I told him.

"While hiking on Neakahne Mountain on Oregon's northern coast I was looking down at the coastline. I saw a man walk from the forest to the Pacific Ocean, so I held up my binoculars to watch him. He waded in the surf for a short time, then returned to the forest. It was not a bear, nor a man. I think it was Bigfoot."

This represents just a few of the many, many Bigfoot stories that have been shared with me by honest people. I think there has been a few jokesters, but most were sober.

Surprisingly while selling my books at a Eugene, Oregon venue, a man came by my table and asked me if I'd like to have a manuscript written about Bigfoot in the 1970s.

I said, "Sure."

The next day he dropped the manuscript on my table. "Here," he said. "It's yours."

I researched the manuscript and found it to be credible. I have since condensed and edited it.

It was written by Ken Coon. He spent 13 years researching and wrote it in the 1970s. The manuscript confirmed what I already knew. In the Pacific Northwest lurks a huge human-like creature that somehow has eluded film and digital cameras, but has left meaningful footprints, and has been seen by countless individuals, including me.

Introduction
by Pat Edwards

Whether or not you believe in the existence of Bigfoot, you will find this book fascinating. Ken Coon truly believed in the work that he spent 13 years of his life doing. His research is detailed and compelling and he has certainly earned my respect.

A career law enforcement officer with the Los Angeles County Sheriff's Department until his retirement in 1973, Ken Coon felt that he was qualified to interview those who reported sightings and determine if their stories were hoaxes. In this book, he presents his reasons:

Are we to believe that all of those loggers, hunters, fishermen, farmers, housewives, students, boy scouts, miners and all the others (who report Bigfoot sightings) are really just publicity-seeking liars? That is a pretty tall order even for a skeptical old cop like me...

I like to believe that I learned something in a quarter century of law enforcement, and one of those things is the ability to interrogate intelligently. Policemen are lied to nearly every day and so, of necessity, must learn techniques of witness interrogation that aid in determining the facts.

As most any good cop might do, immediately after hearing a Bigfoot story, I make it a point to learn what I can about the witness or witnesses. I may have offended some of the witnesses in so doing, but I have always felt it important to learn something of the witness' reputation for honesty, sobriety and stability. The majority of the people in question are residents of rural areas where a reputation as a liar, drunkard or screwball is not likely to be kept secret.

In the great majority of cases, I have found the alleged witness to be of good reputation. In those few cases where I found otherwise, the story had sounded a little fishy, anyway.

Unfortunately, Ken was unable to find a publisher for his manuscript during his lifetime. Following his death, his widow, Beverly, entrusted the manuscript and the accompanying M. Salyers Hamilton illustrations to Ken's good friend, Rick Wohlers, asking him to try to get them published, if possible.

In 2018, upon seeing that Oregon author, Joe Blakely, had written a series of four short novels featuring Bigfoot, Rick approached Joe to see if he would be interested in publishing Ken's work. Joe said that he would see what he could do.

The manuscript was not digitalized and the scans did not convert to Word well, so Joe approached me, his friend and publisher, to help him prepare the book. Our work was quite extensive and we were also left to locate family members for permission to clear any copyright issues.

After a bit of detective work by Rick, Joe and me,

we were finally able to locate a stepdaughter, Dianna Hussman, in California. Her mother had also passed away and as executor of both Ken's and her mother's estate, she issued us the permissions needed to publish the book under Ken's name.

Both Joe and I feel privileged to be able to honor the years of work—the dedication and honest belief—that Ken put into his manuscript.

Whether, upon turning the last page, you accept his hypotheses as facts or even possibilities, or if you prefer to dismiss them as flawed, I am convinced that you, too, will respect the man and his work.

SASQUATCH!
By Ken Coon

Table of Contents

Chapter 1
A Mystery Comes to Light

The date was August 27, 1958. The place was an unfinished logging road deep in the forests of Northern California. It was there that public attention would focus on the phenomenon now known as Bigfoot.

Gerald Crew, a bulldozer operator, was building a logging road into the Bluff Creek area of Northwestern California, a previously untouched wilderness a few miles west of the town of Willow Creek. On the morning of August 28th, Crew discovered enormous footprints in the soft earth near where his caterpillar had been parked for the night. The footprints were approximately 16-inches-long and showed a stride of 46 to 60 inches.

Most of Crew's fellow workers laughed and went on to work, assuming it to be a practical joke. Others were strangely silent and seemed to try to ignore the subject. When further tracks showed up a few nights later, word began to leak out to relatives and friends in the nearby towns of Willow Creek and Orleans.

Then one night, an even stranger thing happened. When the crew reported for work one morning the workmen found that a 55-gallon drum full of diesel oil had been carried up a very steep bank and then thrown into a canyon. A 700-pound tire for an earth-mover had been lifted, rolled and then thrown into the canyon too. The "it" or "who" had also left his giant human-looking tracks all over the place. About this time the press finally began to show an interest. Gerald Crew had taken some casts of the prints. He took them to Andrew Genzoli, editor of the *Humboldt Times* in Eureka. Mr. Genzoli felt that he was on to a story.

He printed pictures of the casts and a report of the recent happenings in Bluff Creek.

Meanwhile, the tracks showed up again on October 2, and continued for three nights. They continued to be seen during the remainder of that fall and winter. Editor Genzoli assigned his reporter Betty Allen to the story. She learned from other workmen that similar things had happened on other jobs in nearby cities.

The name Bigfoot may have originated in these Eureka stories. Formerly the name for Bigfoot had been Sasquatch. For the first time in the United States, Bigfoot was big news, and reached many national newspapers. I became so interested, I did further readings. One excellent writer who investigated the California stories and found them plausible was Ivan T. Sanderson. I later learned that he had written an excellent book called *Abominable Snowmen; Legend Come To Life*, published in 1961. It was Sanderson's book that led me into this fascinating subject of "Sasquatchery." This is when I began my research.

The Early Investigations

As far back as the 1920s, John W. Burns of British Columbia reported his findings on Sasquatch. In fact, it was Burns who created that name, apparently from the Vancouver Island Indian name *Soseq'atl*. Burns was for a number of years a teacher on the Chehalis Indian Reserve on the Harrison River. He published some Sasquatch stories that the Indians had been related to him.

John Green former publisher of the *Agassiz-Harrison Advance* took over where Burns had left off in collecting Canadian Sasquatch stories. Because of his strategic location in the heart of Sasquatch country and his hard-headed determination to "get the facts," Green managed to gather what is surely the largest collection of Sasquatch-Bigfoot reports on file anywhere.

From Burns and Green and other early researchers, we learn that giant, hairy ape-men had been reported from time to time in many areas throughout British Columbia. One of the earliest journal entries, from Canada, goes clear back to 1810. David Thompson, a surveyor and tracker for the Northwest Company described 14½" tracks in deep snow not far from the present sight of Jasper, Alberta. He and his Indian guides were certain that they were not bear tracks.

In 1864, Alexander Caulfield Anderson, an executive of the Hudson's Bay Company, led a survey party into Southern British Columbia looking for trade routes. He reported that he and his men were attacked by giant hairy men who hurled boulders at them from the slopes.

A report was made by a timber cruiser named Mike King, in 1901 from Vancouver Island. King was traveling alone in that rugged country as his Indian guides had refused to continue with him because they were afraid of

3

the "wild men of the woods."

In his sworn statement, King claimed that as he reached the top of a ridge, he saw below him a large reddish-brown creature crouched by the stream. King further related that the creature was washing and stacking roots. Due to its near-human form, King did not fire at the beast as it ran into the brush after catching sight of him. King commented on the animals long arms. King also noted that the tracks it left appeared human-like, but with very long and spreading toes.

Probably the most sensational story ever told about Sasquatch was reported by Albert Ostman, a retired prospector and logger of British Columbia. He reported that in 1924, while on a hunting and prospecting trip into the mountains east of Toba Inlet on the B.C. coast, something very strange happened.

While asleep one night, he was picked up, sleeping bag and all, and carried off by one of the giants. Mr. Ostman described these events in writing and in taped interviews and convinced the investigators he was telling the truth.

Ostman claimed that he was carried some distance in his bag and that when he was finally dumped onto the ground, it was daylight. He found himself in a box canyon and observed that his captor was a huge ape-man. Also present was a large female of similar description and two smaller, partially grown members of the family, one male and one female.

Ostman claimed he was held captive for 7 days at which time he managed to escape and make his way back to civilization.

In that same year, an incident about giant apes

was reported in the Mt. Saint Helens area. A group of prospectors reported seeing four 7-foot-tall hairy "devils." They claimed to have shot and killed one of the creatures, although they never found the body.

That same night their cabin was attacked by someone or something hurling huge boulders on to the roof, virtually destroying it. In making their report, the miners made it clear they were leaving the area and did not plan to return. Shortly thereafter, a posse of newspapermen, lawmen and others proceeded to the area, now known as Ape Canyon. They reported finding huge tracks, but did not see any of the ape-men.

A retired forest ranger who served in the Mt. Saint Helens area told of stories he had heard about the creatures during the 1920s and 30s.

One of the most detailed reports of a sighting is the well-known Chapman case. That occurred in September 1941, outside the little town of Ruby Creek, B.C. The Chapman family lived in a small cabin not far from the Fraser River. About three o'clock one afternoon, one of the Chapman children ran into the house to tell his mother that a bear was coming into the field behind the house. When Mrs.Chapman went out to look, she was startled to observe a giant hairy man-creature approaching. Judging by the nearby fence posts she estimated his height at 7½ -feet. Both she and several of the children had a good look at the creature before they all ran from the house and headed for town.

Later investigation by Mr. Chapman and a number of townspeople disclosed

that the giant had entered a shed and had done considerable damage, which included throwing a 55 gallon tub of fish out the door. The Chapman's never again saw the monster, but foot tracks indicated that he returned to the vicinity of their ranch every night for a week.

All of the reports so far discussed have originated in the heavily forested, mountainous regions of the Northwest. This next incident concerns a sighting that allegedly took place in the arid country of the California-Arizona border. The witness was a respected Los Angeles businessman and requested that his name be withheld. He reported that he was prospecting alone in 1939 when he made the sighting. He states that he was awakened in the middle of the night because of a great fuss being raised by his burro. When he looked out of his sleeping bag to see what was disturbing the animal, he observed an ape-like creature, white in color, attempting to get past the fire, apparently to attack him.

His camp had been made in a sheltered spot in a canyon wall and he had covered it with sagebrush. He had built a fire at the opening of the shelter and he and his burro bedded down behind the fire. Apparently the fire was smaller when he woke and the ape-creature was crouched on the far side of it, fearing the remaining flames.

The witness was armed with a .38 calibre revolver and didn't want to fire at it for fear of infuriating the animal. He then threw more wood on the fire and the creature retreated. At this time the witness observed several similar creatures moving around in the darkness. When the fire burned down, the giants returned and again approached the fire and again the prospector built up the fire, frightening the apes off. After another thirty minutes, the creatures vanished.

The observer described one of the giants as about 6- or 7-feet tall, covered

with long white hair over the body and face. He noted that the eyes glowed red in the firelight. His estimate of the beasts' weight was "over three hundred pounds."

Meanwhile back in Central Oregon during World War II, a couple on a camping trip near Todd Lake reported seeing a giant hairy man. Not long after this sighting, two hunters, O.R. Edwards and Bill Cole reported sighting a giant ape-man in the Siskiyou Mountains of Southwestern Oregon.

The reports so far described are by no means all that have come to my attention from those years, but it was not until after the Bluff Creek incidents received nationwide publicity that reports of the giants began to appear in greater numbers. This does not indicate that there were more of the creatures or that they were more active, but it most likely demonstrates a greater willingness on the part of observers to tell about similar sightings.

An example of that change in attitude might be best illustrated by a letter to the editor of *True Magazine*, following *True*'s publication of a Bigfoot article authored by Ivan Sanderson. The reader thanked True for publishing the article, thereby reassuring him that he had not imagined his encounter with a Bigfoot-type creature some years previously. He stated that he had seen the giant while driving at night on a secondary road near McDoel, California but had not mentioned it to anyone as he had no idea what it was that he had seen.

Through the years, he had almost convinced himself that he had in fact imagined the whole thing. The article in *True* had eased his mind considerably.

An Oregon report from 1959 originated at Tenmile, near Roseburg. In October of that year, two boys, Wayne Johnson and Walter Stork, claimed that they had shot at a huge upright walking, hair-covered monster, with their 30.06 rifle. They stated that they were certain they had hit it—several times—apparently without effect.

The boys' story was investigated by Bob Titmus, who found 11-inch footprints that were extremely wide for their length.

Not long after this sighting, in October 1960, Mr. John Bringsli of Nelson, British Columbia, was berry picking near the head of Lemon Creek when he had a most interesting experience. He looked up form his berry picking to see a 7- to 9-foot tall "apeman" standing on a slight rise watching him. Bringsli stared at the creature for some time, then the giant began walking slowly toward him. That's when Brings decided to leave for other parts and save his berry picking for later.

He described the ape-man as being covered with strange bluish-grey hair and standing on long legs, with short, powerful-looking arms. He also said that it appeared to have no neck, and its ears were flat against the head.

In 1960, an old prospector, Zack Hamilton, left a roll of film in a camera shop for processing. He claimed there was a picture of Bigfoot on the roll. He had taken the shot in the Three Sisters Wilderness Area of Central Oregon. Hamilton never returned for the prints. Several years later, when the Patterson pictures were printed in *Argosy Magazine*, the shop owner opened the package and found the snapshot mentioned by the old timer. It was apparently taken in poor light and with an inexpensive camera showing little detail. The photograph showed the back view of an upright walking gorilla-like creature.

Another report from the year 1960 concerns a fellow named Hatfield who was visiting friends at their home on the outskirts of Fort Bragg, California when he looked out the rear window to see why the dogs were making such a fuss. What he observed was a man-shaped monster or at least the head and shoulders of one, as it looked over the 6-foot fence at the rear of the yard.

When he grabbed a rifle and ran outside, he and the monster ran into each other, knocking Hatfield to the ground. By the time he regained his footing, the monster was gone, but its terrible smell remained for thirty minutes.

That particular incident is especially interesting for two other reasons. First, the 16-inch footprints found in the yard showed only four toes. Next, and perhaps most important, is the giant left a muddy hand-print on the white wall of the house. That enormous print was 11-inches across and human-hand shaped, although the fingers were quite short, proportionately. The finger-prints showed no whorls.

Another extraordinary incident was reported by the owner of a flying service in California. In 1962, Mr. Len Strand and his co-pilot Alden Hoover were flying over the snow-clad Sierra foothills near Twaine Harte when they made their sighting. Mr. Strand described the man-monster to me as being about 10-feet tall, very broad in the shoulders,

with long arms. He stated that it was covered with shaggy, dirty brown hair from head to foot.

When they spotted Bigfoot, it was standing in a snow-covered clearing and turned and ran into the forest as they made their second low pass over the spot. Mr. Hoover took a snapshot from the plane, but it was too blurry and of no value. In August 1963, Charlie Erion, a Washington rancher, found giant tracks along the Lewis River. Those tracks were described as "16- to 18-inches long and human, except way too big..."

A number of other persons viewed those tracks and all agreed that whatever made them had to have come out of the river. The tracks circled out of the river to a nearby dirt road and then returned to the river. There was no evidence of a boat having landed nearby. It it interesting to note that just a few days earlier, a family in a fishing boat had reported a 10-foot, beige-colored giant that they had seen standing near the edge of the same river. The giant had lumbered into the forest upon the approach of the boat.

Not only have an ever-increasing number of reports come to light since 1968, but strangely enough, there has been a very notable increase in the apparent area of Bigfoot habitat. Rather than originating almost exclusively from the Pacific Northwest, a sizable percentage of the reports since 1958 have come from other parts of the country. There is no doubt, certainly, that much of this interesting trend can be attributed to the fact that as time has gone by, more and more investigators have searched out and compiled reports in areas that had not previously been investigated.

By the early 1960s, although the majority of reports were still emanating from the Northwest, some reports were coming in from Montana, Idaho, Arizona and even Southern California. I had also learned of a sighting by a man named Dione Pollard who had seen a Sasquatch and tracks in the Diamond Mountains of Nevada.

With the reports of tracks and sightings of these

strange and unknown creatures originating from so many areas, it is an interesting turn of fate that allowed Roger Patterson to take the first real photographic evidence from the very locality where the whole thing started, Bluff Creek, California. It was in the bed of Bluff Creek not far from where Jerry Crew saw the tracks that Roger Patterson says he obtained his photographic evidence. The dispute over the authenticity of the film still rages.

According to Roger, he and his friend Bob Gimlin were riding upstream alongside Bluff Creek when they suddenly sighted a female Bigfoot kneeling next to the stream-bed. Upon sighting the creature, the horses reared and both Patterson and his horse fell. In the meantime, the Bigfoot stood up, turned and ran toward the forest. Patterson scrambled to his feet and was able to get a few feet of film as the creature fled. I have had the opportunity to examine the film and have been to the location where it was supposed to have been taken. These photographs are well-known to the general public by now, so a detailed description is unnecessary at this point. As anyone who has seen the pictures can tell, the creature appears to be a large, thickset, upright-walking primate, covered with long dark hair.

From the late 1960s to date, there has been a veritable flood of reports relating to encounters with hairy monsters or of discovery of giant man-like footprints. Interestingly, the scene of greatest Bigfoot activity seems to shift from time to time. In the winter of 1969-70 it centered around the village of Bossburg, Washington, on the banks of the Columbia River. In just a few months, in 1973, over one hundred reports came from Central Pennsylvania. As this is written, the majority of reports reaching me are coming from Antelope Valley California, 75 miles north of Los Angeles.

The evidence that we have monsters among us is a great deal more than a few melted impressions in the snow and some tall tales told by "drunken loggers," as one anthropologist remarked. Giant hairy, man-like creatures have been frightening the very devil out of people here in North America since long before the arrival of the white man. The creatures, whatever they may be, have been reported by sober, sane and sincere people in nearly every state in the U.S. and in all of the Western Canadian provinces.

Although as this is written, no Bigfoot has yet been brought in for study. It is now clearly obvious that several races of unknown, man-like primates inhabit the wilds of North America.

Chapter 2

The Search

A brief re-counting of my own efforts and adventures in the search for solutions to the mystery.

It seemed simple enough, really. After reading that "Abominable Snowmen" were nearly as close as my own backdoor, I felt it would be easy enough to have a look at one for myself and perhaps obtain a photograph or two.

I had been a professional law enforcement officer for many years and felt I was a fair woodsman as well. I really believed that with the skills learned in those two activities I could almost certainly be successful. After a dozen years, I am still trying, although I'm beginning to suspect that it may be a bit more difficult than I had imagined it to be.

In law enforcement, we take the direct approach to any problem and that seemed the answer here. We know that if a particular type of crime is being committed frequently in a specific area, the most practical step to take is to flood the area with patrolmen or in some cases with a number of detectives, on stake-out. If the criminal or criminals continue to operate in the same area, it is only a matter of time until criminal and officer meet under circumstances that lead, hopefully, to the arrest of the offender.

Bigfoot seemed to make his appearance in certain areas of Northwestern California from time to time, so I decided to go there and have a look. My theory was that if I was in his neighborhood often enough, it would be only a matter of time before we crossed paths. Many persons unfamiliar with the great forests of the Northwest have expressed this same thought— "Why not just go up there and hang around that canyon until you see one?"

I failed to take into account the nature of the country, that incredibly rugged, heavily forested and really quite extensive area that was in those days referred to as "Bigfoot Country."

In the summer of 1962, I made a preliminary tour of the localities in Northwestern California where Sanderson had reported things of interest. For those unfamiliar with that region, let me say that the country is simply overwhelming. I remember my first view from a high spot in the area. I could look thirty or forty miles north to Oregon, thirty miles west to the Pacific Ocean and east to Mt. Shasta. To the south was a seemingly endless series of mountains and canyons. These same mountains and rugged canyons seemed to fill every inch of space in all directions and they were covered with the most unbelievably dense canopy of forest I had ever seen. As hopeless as my project seemed, the thought that very possibly there were giant man-animals lurking in some of those canyons made me determined to find one.

The Little People

It's not that I intended to start small, it just worked

out that way. In late summer of 1962, my son Doug and I spent a week backpacking through the Bluff Creek area, without coming across any Bigfoot sign. On our return trip, we spent a few days further south, including one night camped on the Mad River. We had followed a logging road to the river through some very heavily-forested country. Upon arrival at the point where the road crosses the river, we located a suitable camping spot a few hundred yards from the road, and right on the sandy bank of the river.

As we arrived at the camp sight I observed two things... First, that someone, apparently fishermen, had camped there recently and also that there were several sets of small footprints imbedded in the sand. I will admit to more than a little excitement as I examined the prints and found them to be nearly human in shape, just under 4½-inches long, and with very narrow, pointed heels!

Doug, at the time an active member of the Boy Scouts, scoffed at the whole thing, pointing out that they were most likely the prints of porcupine. It was getting dark, but I did take time to measure and sketch the prints before setting up camp.

Our camp activities destroyed most of the prints, but the next morning I had a better look at what few were left. There appeared to be several sets of them and what or whoever had made them had emerged directly from the river, proceeded to the abandoned camp sight and had dug up some buried trash. The prints then returned to the river. If made by four-legged animals, then they were either walking on hind legs only or all four feet were identical. No claw marks were visible and no tail-drag marks.

Upon our return home, I checked a field book of

North American mammals and indeed the prints did look somewhat like the hind paw prints of the porcupine. Keep in mind, however, that the Mad River prints had no front paw marks and no claw marks. I did find one drawing of some prints similar to what we had seen. On page 469 of Sanderson's Abominable Snowmen was a similar print labeled... Human (*Malayan Negrito*).

The memory of those tiny prints still bothers me.

If they were made by porcupines, then the Mad River Valley has some of the strangest acting porkies in the world.

If made by human children, then they too had some strange habits. They apparently swam to the spot along this secluded section of river, as there was no evidence of a boat. They then proceeded to scratch around an abandoned camp and returned the way they came. Also odd, is the fact that the several individuals involved all had the same unusual foot shape, amounting to a deformity, were they human children.

In late summer of 1963, I returned to Bluff Creek— but this time alone. I know from experience that one sees and hears a great deal more wildlife when moving slowly through the forest, alone.

I used the Fish Lake Campground as a base of operations, as it is on the Bluff Creek Road, several miles off of Highway 96. It was, at the time, a primitive camp, seldom used even in summer. When I arrived, the summer season was over and I was alone there for the entire week—or at least I thought I had been until something occurred the last day which caused me to wonder.

I had spent most of each day for a week, investigating the area in and around Bluff Creek and was preparing to leave. I decided to take one last walk up a small canyon, whose stream empties into Fish Lake. I was gone only a few minutes, as I was somewhat concerned with a mechanical problem on my automobile and wanted to be in civilization before dark. I had followed a narrow animal trail up the canyon and upon my return trip noticed what at first appeared to be a child's barefoot print in one of the few spots on the trail where the surface was suitable for footprint impressions.

This discovery was really quite startling because it was obvious that the print had been recently placed over my boot print. Yet, so far as I was aware, there was no one in the vicinity nor had there been for the week that I had been there. I had not seen or heard anyone and I am certain it would have been quite impossible for a vehicle to approach the campgrounds without my hearing or seeing it. The only road leading to the camp is Bluff Creek road. It's rough dirt and very dusty.

Whoever made that tiny print had obviously walked up the trail just after I had. By no stretch of the imagination can I believe that a family drove up that long, rough road, stopped to let their children play for a few minutes, then drove silently away. To do so would have required a completely silent vehicle, children who were deaf mutes and parents who were willing to let their child or children run barefoot in rough country known for its large rattlesnakes. One other thing—their child had the strangest-looking foot, quite narrow and pointed at the heel!

This was really becoming quite exasperating; two trips in search of giants and all I had found had been some very strange looking child's prints. On many field trips since, I have wished that I could do as well.

I continued this same pattern of informal field trips during the summer of 1964. Due to my eagerness and limited vacation time, I had spent little time interviewing people in the nearby towns, preferring to learn what I could by mail. It was then that I received my first lessons on the subject of unanswered letters, a problem that seems to plague all Bigfoot hunters. I wrote to certain individuals in the area as well as several governmental agencies. I invariably have better luck with the latter as far as answers are concerned. The Trinity County Sheriff's Department answered that they were aware of the Bigfoot reports, but had not made any official investigation. They also mentioned that a scientist from the East had been there several years before asking questions. That was most certainly Ivan Sanderson.

Through the years, all of my contacts with the U.S. Forest Service have been most pleasant, and the employees, polite and helpful. In the summer of 1964, I wrote asking for information on the subject of Bigfoot reports as well as some advice as to the more remote areas of the Six Rivers National Forest. I still have the letter in response, written in a friendly, yet tongue-in cheek vein, pointing out that such reports of monsters are common in many parts of the world and pointing out that some people believe in anything, even Santa Claus. The official who wrote the letter did include a map with the more remote areas of the national forest marked on it. He circled several areas that he said were, for all practical purposes, unknown to the Forest Service.

Like everyone that I had questioned on the subject up to that time, he had never seen any of the footprints, but knew someone who claimed they had. He then related that a crew working on a Jeep trail near Elk Valley had reported prints the previous summer in the soft earth around their equipment.

Due to the fact that the latest information regarding tracks was what I had learned from the Forest Service, I headed for Elk Valley, which is directly north of Bluff Creek. The headwaters of many of the creeks in the area are to be found near Elk Valley; Bluff Creek among them. Because the country was particularly rugged and remote, I felt it unwise to spend ten days in there alone, I took with me Dean Sebree and Roger Munn, two good friends. Dean has had considerable big game hunting experience and is an excellent tracker. Roger is an experienced woodsman who has spent considerable time in the mountains alone. Among other things, he has backpacked alone over most of the famous Muir Trail of the Sierras.

Elk Valley shows on the map as a forestry station, which it is not. Actually it is simply a meadow at the end of the logging road that winds for so many miles through the forest from the town of Orleans. Nearby Sawtooth Peak is the high spot in the Klamath area and from there it is possible to look down into Bluff Creek. We also searched the Blue Creek area from the headwaters for several miles south as this was one of the locations noted by the Forest Service as most primitive. We spent several days down in that canyon without ever coming across any sign that another human had ever been there. Although there are many places in the Northwest seldom visited by man, you can almost be sure that if anyone has been there, some old beer cans or cigarette packages will have been left as evidence.

We became discouraged by our lack of success in the Elk Valley, Blue Creek area, so we headed back to civilization. We decided to see what we might learn from the local inhabitants. Upon questioning people in the nearby towns, we learned that some footprints had been reported in the Hyampom area. Hyampom is a little fishing and lumbering town on the south fork of the Trinity River, about forty miles southeast of Bluff Creek.

The answers we received from the proprietor of the general store in Hyampom were typical of those we heard time and again in those days. They had never seen any of the tracks and did not really believe in the Bigfoot, but the proprietor did know people who had seen tracks. As usual, those who did believe were loggers or road workers who had come across the giant footprints on the job.

At the Hyampom ranger station we talked with the forestry officers who all denied ever having seen any of the tracks, but each of them seemed to know someone who had. That type of statement was typical of Forest Service employees at that time, but as we shall see, they have had a bit more to say in recent years—unofficially, at least.

After a brief look around the Hyampom backroads, we gave up our Bigfoot hunting for another year. At this point in time I had never met anyone else seriously involved in a search for the giants. I assumed that others had been stimulated to action by Sanderson's book, and of course, that was true, but most of the early investigators were doing their work on a purely individual basis, as I was. It was in 1965 that I first learned of the efforts of Lee Trippett of Eugene, Oregon. A newspaper article on the Bigfoot subject had mentioned his name. In corresponding with him I learned of his extensive investigation into the mystery, which in turn made me painfully aware that my own efforts to this point had been not only casual, but quite unscientific in nature.

It was now dawning on me that "catching up with Bigfoot" was going to require more than a leisurely field trip during vacation periods. In the summer of 1965, I organized the first of several well-equipped and fully-staffed expeditions.

For this first expedition, I chose four acquaintances of mine, each of whom possessed skills that would be of value to the expedition. Morris Bowman had successfully hunted nearly every species of big game in North America. Even though our intentions toward Bigfoot were peaceful in nature I felt it would be wise to have Morris along, properly armed, in case Bigfoot's intentions proved somewhat more violent than our own.

The next expedition member chosen was Dr. C.E.O. "Bud" Clever, an experienced backpacker and outdoorsman. Bud has the sharpest eyes of any woodsman I know.

The remaining two party members were Andy Kuchta, amateur naturalist and Bob Briley, who lays claim to the self-assigned title of "World's Finest Camp Cook."

We gathered an impressive array of photographic equipment and some experimental devices designed to attract the creatures within camera range. Equipped with new four-wheel-drive vehicles and camping gear, we headed for the Bluff Creek area in late August, 1965.

We learned from the Forest Service at Orleans that prints had been reported within the last two weeks at a place called Laird Meadow which is only a couple of miles from Bluff Creek,and within the same general area where most of the prints had been found in past years.

Upon arrival at the meadow, we found some good-sized bear tracks that had possibly been responsible for the Bigfoot track report. Using Laird Meadow as a base camp, we searched the rugged, heavily-forest countryside in all directions during the following three weeks. Our modus operandi was to search until we found fresh tracks then set up our Bigfoot lures in an attempt to bring the creature within camera range.

One day while following a stream down a small side canyon we began noticing some strange things, none of which, individually, would have meant anything to us, but together caused us to look even more closely. First there were impressions on the side of the bank where it appeared that a very heavy animal had walked and slid down the side. A bear perhaps, but the impressions seemed much too long for bear tracks. Then we noticed something else, this same heavy creature had apparently broken off the top of a small tree—small, that is, for that area, but several inches in diameter. It was broken off about 6-feet from the ground. There were no claw marks; just a clean break. We admitted to ourselves that we might be using our imaginations just a little, but it did look like Bigfoot had come down the bank, started to slide and had used the small tree as a brace, breaking the tree with his great weight. Whatever had happened, it had occurred some months earlier.

As we continued on downstream, Doc Clever's sharp eyes spotted several other impressions in the soil near the stream bank. They certainly did have the size and general outline of Bigfoot prints, but were not distinct enough for casting. Also, they just might have been natural depressions in the soil, or so we thought, until we found one that was obviously a Bigfoot print. It, too, had been made in the springtime, while the soil was still wet, and it had leaves and pine needles dried in it. The toes were visible and the general shape and proportions of the prints compared very closely with a cast we were to see a few days later.

Doc Clever made an effort to cast the print with plaster of paris but it did not turn out as well as we would have liked due to the leaves and pine needles imbedded in it. Removing them would have further destroyed the outlines of the print.

A couple of days later, we observed on the sloping, muddy shore of nearby Onion Lake, where some creature had stepped and slid in the mud. Due to the obvious sliding of the foot, the print was distorted but whatever had made the print must have had a very large, oblong foot.

A careful study of the print showed no claw marks and no signs of a boot heel. Whatever had made the gigantic print had been there within the last day or two. We then made several night excursions in the area of the lake, but without success.

An old prospector maintains a cabin not far from Onion Lake. We stopped by to talk with him on several occasions. Because he had spent many summers in the area, we hoped to learn something about Bigfoot from him.

As he was the only resident of that locality, we felt that he probably had a great deal to tell us if he would.

In our first conversation with him, he admitted seeing the tracks at the Bluff Creek construction site in 1958. He stated that he felt they were a hoax. In one of our later conversations with him, he did relate an interesting experience. Some years before, the exact year unknown, but before the Bluff Creek road was constructed. He had been packing out over an old Indian trail at the end of the summer season, when a light, early snow began to fall. As he hurried down the trail toward civilization, he was surprised to see human footprints in the trail. Especially surprising was the fact that the lone traveler was obviously barefooted and was heading back up into the high country.

His first thought had been to attempt to overtake the mystery hiker as he felt he was some sort of greenhorn who was lost and heading the wrong way, considering the weather. He thought better of the idea, though, when upon closer inspection of the tracks, he noted that they were about twice the size of his, the stride at least twice the length of his own and the tracks were "kind of funny looking."

As our time ran out, we headed toward home, somewhat disappointed that we still had not observed one of the monsters. We were pleased, of course, with the fact that we had at last found some fairly good prints as evidence.

On our return trip, we stopped by Al Hodgson's variety store in Willow Creek. Al was becoming quite well-known locally for his interest in the Bigfoot mystery. We were told that Al had a good Bigfoot print cast we should see.

We were quite pleasantly surprised when we examined and measured Al's cast as it was apparently made by the same foot as the print we had cast.

In the nearby town of Weaverville, we had a long talk with the curator of the Trinity County Museum. We learned from him that there are several references to

Bigfoot in old Trinity County newspapers of the Gold Rush era.

The Sierras

Several recent reports of monster sightings had come from the western slope of California's Sierra Nevada mountains, in what is often called the Mother Lode Country. In the spring of 1966, I went into that area to look it over and to check on some of the reports.

I spoke with a deputy sheriff in the resort village of Pinecrest who stated he had seen huge footprints in the snow near there. He said that who or whatever it was, had apparently been running down a snow-covered slope with a 12-foot stride!

This same officer related how he and his partner had been contacted by a party of loggers one night who insisted that "they get a bunch of guys with guns and come back to our camp." The reason for the request was that they had seen a "horrible-looking monster," near their campfire, in the forest several miles south of Pinecrest.

The officers did accompany the men back to their camp, but found no evidence of the creature.

The following day I spoke with Len Strand, owner of the Columbia Flying Service in the old frontier town of Columbia. Strand was a sober, intelligent and serious businessman who was more than a little reluctant to tell of his sighting. He had suffered considerable ridicule after his report had reached the papers. When I finally convinced him of the sincerity of my interest, he described in detail the giant, upright walking, fur-covered man-like thing he and his partner had observed while flying over a snow-covered hillside near the town of Twain Harte.

Later that summer, Doctor Clever and I went into the Immigrant Gap Primitive Area nearby and at a higher elevation from where these reports had emanated. We reasoned that since those sightings and tracks had been made during a winter of very heavy snowfall, the creature or creatures had moved down from the more remote primitive area due to the weather. We were unsuccessful in obtaining any evidence, but once again it was a matter of too little time and too much country.

Evidence Of A Different Kind

During our 1965 expedition into the Bluff Creek area, we had found our first Bigfoot evidence, although the only tracks we had been certain of, appeared to be several months old. We felt that the heavy logging operation taking place in the area might have driven the creatures farther back into the higher country. Because the logging was still in progress in the summer of 1966, we decided to go farther north, beyond where the loggers were working. Some miles north of Bluff Creek, and just south of the Oregon border is a string of small lakes extending from near the headwaters of the Smith River, east to near the Elk Valley that we had visited several years previously. Just exactly how many lakes there are is a question even the Forest Service could not answer and the maps do not all agree. The area had not, at that time, ever been thoroughly surveyed and the location of lakes, streams and peaks is sometimes not accurate as indicated on the maps.

The 1966 expedition was organized and equipped in much the same manner as the 1965 Bluff Creek effort had been, although several additional personnel had been included for this later trip.

On our way into the high lake country, we spent a few days on Wooley Creek, some miles northeast of Bluff Creek. A patient of Doc Clever's had related to him a most interesting story concerning Wooley Creek. He had told the doctor that several years earlier, while on a fishing trip, one of the party had come across gigantic bare, human-like footprints in the wet sand.

It was up Wooley Creek that the first of a series of unfortunate incidents occurred that plagued us for this entire trip. One of our men, while fording the stream, fell into a deep hole and very nearly drowned. He was fortunate enough to escape with only a soaked gun, camera and binoculars to show for his mishap.

We spent only two days on Wooley Creek before heading on northwest to the lake country on the Oregon border. The Wooley Creek area is wild and beautiful and deserved a much closer look than our limited time allowed.

When we reached the area of the lakes, we set up base camp at Sanger Lake and commenced exploring the nearby canyons. Near Raspberry Lake, about a half-day's hike from Sanger, we came upon an apparently fresh pile of feces that was somewhat human-like except for its great size. There were many examples of bear feces nearby as the bears had apparently congregated around the lake because the raspberries were ripe. The color and shape of the bear droppings was quite different from the example we photo- graphed. The example in question was quite different in color, shape and consistency. We made no effort to carry the material to a medical lab for examination as we were at least two days travel from a proper laboratory. Another reason for our reluctance to leave with the evidence was the fact that the feces seemed very fresh and we fully expected to come upon a hairy giant around the next bend in the trail!

As it turned out, we did leave the area a few days later. This trip had been jinxed with bad luck from the start. Our crew member who had fallen into the creek and nearly drowned, later had a close call when his revolver accidentally discharged, striking the outside edge of the boot on his right foot. Morris Bowman had developed the most serious case of poison oak rash any of us had ever seen, and though we all had suggested remedies, none seemed to help. He and Dean Sebree decided to return home and then when the weather suddenly turned cold and wet, we all decided to give it up for the year.

Bigfoot Hunting By Canoe

Because of the many accidents and unfortunate incidents that had occurred on the big expedition the previous year. Doc Clever and I decided to return to a two-man operation for 1967. There is—or was—a stretch of the Klamath River country in Northern California that could only be reached by water. It is a heavily-forested area just south of the Bluff Creek country and we were determined to have a look at it. In the spring of 1967, we spent three days and two nights on the river. Although we discovered the tracks of many types of wildlife on the banks and sandbars, we found no Bigfoot evidence.

Roger Patterson, a Yakima, Washington, horse rancher and Bigfoot buff had recently published a book, *Do Abominable Snowmen of America Really Exist?* and I was beginning to wonder if he or someone else would come up with some real proof of the giants before I did.

Because we felt the fecal evidence we had found the previous year was the freshest evidence we had yet come across, Doc and I returned to that area at the same time of year that we had been there in 1966. We had no luck at all and gave it up after ten days of searching the lakes region. We discussed returning to the Bluff Creek area for another try, but decided to give up for the year as we felt there was too much logging activity still going on there. We returned home and it was just a month later that Roger Patterson filmed the female Bigfoot at Bluff Creek.

In the last couple of years, we had developed the habit of stopping at each Forest Service station in "Bigfoot Country" to ask about possible Bigfoot reports and to ascertain the attitudes and opinions of the rangers.

During the 1967 trip, we had begun to notice a change in attitude of the Forest Service people. Many of them were obviously beginning to accept the fact that there was "something" in those forests that the textbooks had not mentioned.

We had frequently heard the name "Syl McCoy" mentioned as the forestry employee who was most expert on the subject of Bigfoot tracks. We had stopped in to see him on our way home in 1967 and he had told us that he had found many tracks in the Hyampom area, along the south fork of the Trinity River from time to time. For that reason we decided to try the south fork in 1968. Actually, that was not the only reason... We felt that Bluff Creek would be overrun with monster seekers, due to the publicity the Patterson film had caused. However, after more than a week in the Hyampom area we could not resist returning to Bluff Creek, crowds or no crowds.

As it turned out, we were in error, expecting Bluff Creek to be full of Bigfoot hunters as a result of the publicity given Patterson's film. We did come across a couple in a four-wheel-drive vehicle who claimed to be collecting flowers for the Smithsonian. We saw them or their tracks several times, but did not find any evidence that they were gathering botanical specimens, although they were acting very much like Bigfoot hunters.

There was also said to be a crew from the British Broadcasting Company, "staked out" there on Bigfoot, but we never did see them.

Although it was now early May, the roads were impassable in some places because of snowdrifts. We soon ran out of time and had to return home, realizing once again that hunting Bigfoot should be a full-time occupation.

A Conference of Sasquatchers

In June of the same year, Al Hodgson notified me that John Green was bringing the Patterson film to Willow Creek and that a number of others interested in the search would be there. Not only because of the opportunity to see the film, but also to meet Green and the others, Bob Critchlow and I flew to Willow Creek on the 22nd. I particularly wanted to take Bob along because he had shown a definite interest in Sasquatchery, but still seemed to have an open mind, not really believing or disbelieving.

I was impressed by the fact that he came away fully convinced that Bigfoot was real by the pictures and the casts he had seen and the discussions he had heard. Bob has been a detective for nearly two decades and possesses a truly incisive and analytical mind.

The film was shown in the Willow Creek school auditorium and a good many of the townspeople were there. As Hodgson pointed out, though, some of the most vocal non-believers had remained absent, apparently not even willing to expose themselves to the possibility of having their minds changed.

After the showing, a group of serious Bigfooters gathered at Syl McCoy's home and exchanged information. It was a valuable two hours and I only wish now that I had taped it. No doubt, in years to come, many similar meetings will be held, attended by persons of far more impressive academic backgrounds than ours, but this meeting was impressive. It was doubtless the first time in history that a number of Sasquatch researchers had ever gathered for the purpose of exchanging information.

The following day, Green led a number of us to the spot in Bluff Creek where Patterson's pictures were taken.

The depressions were still visible in the sand, where the giant apparently had run along the sandbank while being photographed. This spot is about three miles northwest of where we took our casts in 1965 and is only about two miles upstream from where the whole excitement started in 1958.

Nevada

From time to time, I had been receiving bits and pieces of information from Nevada, relative to Bigfoot sightings. I received an interesting report from a rancher near Eureka, Nevada. In looking over the maps and after flying over the area, it seemed most unlikely, as the location of the sighting was a barren mountain in a semi-arid region. However, after receiving rumors of still another sighting in the same area, we decided to have a look into that country. The only range of mountains nearby that seemed to have sufficient water and vegetation was the Ruby Mountains, just south of Elko and a few miles north of Eureka.

We took a large and well-equipped group into the Rubies.

For the first time, we included a professional photographer, but as it turned out, he had nothing to photograph. My idea had been that rather than search the whole northeastern part of this huge state, we should restrict ourselves to the Ruby range, on the assumption that the other sightings had been made while "the Ridgewalker" had been on tour of the countryside. We talked to road workers, rangers, fish and game people and old-time ranchers who were familiar with the Rubies, but none had ever seen anything.

Doc Clever and I packed into some high country (10,400 feet) in the snow, but found nothing. After getting a good look at Northeastern Nevada, we realized that although the terrain is semi-arid, there is sufficient vegetation, even on the valley floors, to provide food and even some cover for a Bigfoot-type creature. There are many hundreds of square miles of that country that is dotted with small ranges of hills or mountains with water and a surprising amount of vegetation. Once again, we found ourselves faced with the familiar problem; too much country and too little time.

I had now been involved in the search for seven years.

My associates and I traveled hundreds of miles by four-wheel-drive vehicle in the back country. We hiked and backpacked through some of the most heavily-forested country in the U.S. We took every possible day from our jobs and our families to devote to the search. The total result of all that effort was the discovery of a few funny looking "little people" tracks, a few indistinct probable Bigfoot prints, and a pile of odd-looking dung.

By this time I had begun corresponding with a number of other Bigfoot seekers including George Haas, John Green, Jim McClarin and Lee Trippett. Although reports of sightings and tracks were still trickling into our files, none of us were having any luck in solving the mystery of the "what is it" of the northwest forests.

Even Patterson's film had accomplished little toward encouraging scientific investigation into the matter. After still another unsuccessful excursion into the Bluff Creek area in 1969, I had about decided to give up Sasquatching for some more profitable pastime.

Enthusiasm was suddenly re-kindled when sighting reports began coming in from the Oroville area of northeastern California. The creatures—at least two of them, apparently a female and a young—had made repeated appearances in a rural area just a few miles north of Oroville.

Oroville first became the center for Bigfoot hunters activities as a result of the report of Charles Jackson, owner of a ranch about six miles from Oroville and not far from the great Oroville Dam. Jackson told authorities that on the afternoon of July 12, 1969, he and his son had been burning rubbish when they sighted a Bigfoot standing just a few feet away, near the barn. He described the creature as 7- to 8-feet tall, covered with grey hair and with very large breasts.

A few days later, retired army officer, Homer Stickly, reported sighting a huge, upright creature walking across his meadow. The Stickly place is less than a mile from the Jackson home. As a result of those two reports and several others from the same general vicinity during the summer of 1969, a number of investigators spent considerable time in and around Oroville, particularly on the Stickly ranch. Roger Patterson, Jim McClarin and others reported finding tracks and of hearing screams, but all eventually gave up and moved on to other areas.

I had been following the Oroville reports with keen interest, but was unable to spend even a few days there because of job responsibilities. Finally in January 1970, I made a hurried trip there with Bill Early and Lou Zaninovitch as companions.

Finding Bigfoot Evidence Is Easy!

Bill Early was a young deputy marshal who had looked me up when he heard that I was a Bigfoot researcher. He had been tremendously interested in the subject for some time, but had never pursued the matter in the field. After a brief trip with him to Bluff Creek the previous year, I knew Bill to be an excellent companion on the trail and one of the most humorous people I have ever known. In the years since, we have spent many hundreds of pleasant hours in search of solutions to the great mystery. Lou Zaninovitch, a friend of Bill's had just come along out of curiosity.

There had been continued Bigfoot activity in the Oroville area throughout the summer and fall of 1969, but it had decreased considerably by the time we got there. To add to our problems, the area had suffered severe rains for more than a week prior to our arrival.

We drove first to the Stickly home and found Mr. and Mrs. Stickly eager to discuss the Bigfoot activity in and around their property. They stated that on a number of occasions, one or more of the creatures had apparently walked up the slope behind their home and then crossed the road, continuing on through the meadow where Mr. Stickly had seen the giant the previous summer. They reported that their two full-grown shepherd dogs always reacted with signs of great fear at such times, refusing to leave the house. Mrs. Stickly also mentioned that the night visitors had made her horse so nervous that she had been unable to ride it for several months.

After leaving the Stickly's, we proceeded down into the meadow and within just a few minutes we came across two sets of very fresh, very large footprints. The prints in the mud had apparently been made within the past hour, possibly during the time that we were visiting the Sticklys. They showed no evidence of having been rained upon and heavy rain had been falling until a short time before we had arrived at the Stickly place.

Those were the first really fresh Bigfoot tracks I had seen and the sight of them was a bit of a shock. Of the two series of tracks, one was apparently made by a foot 15 inches long. The smaller tracks alongside measured about 9 inches. Despite the grass and very wet mud, toe impressions were clearly visible in some of the prints. Somehow a 15-inch print, or a Bigfoot print of any size, for that matter, is not nearly so impressive in a photograph as when seen in its natural state. The depth of the tracks was astonishing, when compared to the depth of the track made by my own 200 pounds. It's one thing to read and talk about 8 foot, 900 pound monsters, but it is something else again to see fresh, very fresh, evidence of the creatures right before your eyes. The tracks, about two dozen of them, continued on down an oak-covered hillside, along a fence line and through an opening in the fence. From there they faded out after entering brushy, rocky terrain. We spent the rest of the day cautiously searching for more evidence, hoping and really expecting to run into the creatures at any time. We spent several more days and nights in the immediate area without further luck. This had been our first opportunity to put out our Bigfoot enticement devices. There was certainly no doubt in our minds that at least two of the creatures were or had very recently been in the immediate vicinity. In fact, I will never forget Lou's comment that, "This Bigfoot stuff is a cinch. We found all those tracks in only a few minutes after we started looking!"

It did seem a bit incredible to us to have found two sets of footprints only a few hundred yards off of a paved road and only six miles from a good-sized city. Particularly so, after 8 years of really rugged excursions into the deep forest of northwestern California had brought us so little return.

Several subsequent field trips to the same area failed to provide us with any additional, positive evidence. On one occasion, my two sons, accompanied by several of their buddies, were searching the area of some caves near the edge of a butte, about a mile from where we had found the tracks.

They reported hearing heavy footfalls and crashing brush. They also noted a most foul odor in the area, but a diligent search failed to reveal any signs of what might have caused the odor and the sounds. There have been a few reports from the Oroville area since that time, but none of the regular, frequent activity that had been occurring in 1970. I can well-imagine that the Sticklys are not the least bit sorry about that.

In the summer of 1970, an area near Platina, California began to attract the attention of Bigfooters. Platina is just a few miles east of Hyampom where so much Bigfoot activity had been reported in previous years. George Haas and John Dana had found 16-inch tracks in the area in July 1969. In the following months several sightings had been reported in and near the public campground at Basin Gulch, not far from Platina. Investigator Archie Buckly had reported that on May 14th , he had seen, by flashlight at 3:00 a.m., a 7-foot-tall creature with glowing eyes. The next day, he found 15-inch tracks.

Ben Foster, a Bigfoot hunter from Anderson, California, had reported that he and his wife had, on several occasions, seen two of the creatures near the Basin Gulch campground at dusk.

Shortly after the Foster sightings, Bill Early and I spent a few days at Basin Gulch. On our first day at the camp, Ben took us up a nearby canyon and pointed out several indistinct tracks about 16 inches long. Upon our return to camp, I discovered a most startling sight! Something or someone with a 60-inch stride had walked through camp, between Bill's vehicle and the tent, leaving 16-inch-long footprints, deeply impressed in the fir needle mulch of the forest floor. The tracks had not been seen by any of us prior to leaving camp and almost certainly were made during our two-hour absence.

If the thought of a giant wild man walking through a public campground in broad daylight is not incredible enough, consider the fact that the campground is located less than a mile from a paved highway and is almost within sight of the Basin Gulch Ranger Station.

Although tracks found in some remote canyon in a vast forest area are hardly suspect, we were certainly suspicious of these tracks, found right where a hoaxer would know they would be found. The hoax idea fails to hold up, in my opinion, when we note that the tracks were imbedded very deeply into the forest floor, leaving a permanent impression, something we found it impossible to do, even by jumping on the mulch, wearing heavy boots. Whoever or whatever made the footprints obviously had very long legs and weighed many hundreds of pounds.

In the following days and nights, other things occurred that led us to believe that one or more of the giants were frequenting the immediate vicinity of our camp. One evening in particular, as we were all sitting around the fire, someone commented that it had become suspiciously quiet; even the crickets had become strangely silent. We then heard movement among the trees on the hillside immediately above camp. We all sat motionless for a long time, without seeing anything. Finally, Ben shined a flashlight on the hillside, but we did not observe anything—even the deer we had really expected to see. The following morning we found a number of large impressions in the soft soil of the hillside above camp. From a study of the impressions, it appeared that one or more of the giants had moved quite close to our camp and had traveled from tree to tree to remain out of sight.

We returned to Basin Gulch from time to time from 1970 to 1973 but without any further success. George Haas and his group have spent most of the past three summers there. One additional sighting had been reported to them and they had collected some evidence; however, they had not been successful in observing one of the beasts and George's complex array of camera traps had not yet put Bigfoot on film.

By 1972, about the only thing that had not changed in Bigfooting was the mystery itself. The public, the Forest Service and even a few anthropologists were evincing a change in attitude about the whole thing. Where I had once felt quite alone in the search, it now seemed that dozens of individuals and quite a number of organizations had taken up the search for answers to the great riddle. By 1972, I was corresponding with Green, Dahindin, Haas, McLarin and a number of other researchers throughout the west and northwest. Also, mainly due to the *Bigfoot Bulletin* published by George Haas, I frequently heard from interested people who had read my name in the bulletin. Because I was living in Southern California it was logical that anyone with a Bigfoot story from that area would contact me.

Bill and I had conducted some investigations into reports originating in the mountains and deserts of Southern California. It seemed totally illogical at first, that giant man-apes might be living in the semi-arid southwest, but as time went by we were forced to change our opinions.

A Los Angeles businessman related his experience with several "big white apes" that had approached his camp on the Mojave Desert in 1939.

A school teacher and his wife related to me how they had fled at the approach of a "huge hairy ape-man" while they had been picnicking at the mouth of a canyon near Hesperia.

A young lady visiting our home noted a footprint cast and stated that she and some friends had seen similar footprints while hiking in the foothills near Palmdale.

Even all of this background had not prepared me for the letter I received from a young man named Joel Hurd. Joel, in his early twenties, was deeply involved in the ecology craze. His interest in the ecology situation had led him into the subject of Bigfoot and he had an interesting idea. Because Bigfoot seemed to be a big, harmless wild fellow, why wouldn't he make an excellent symbol for the ecology project? Somewhat like Smoky Bear has been for fire prevention. In order to push his idea he became involved in research with the hopes that he could prove that there were really such creatures. His efforts in that direction had resulted in a most interesting discovery. He had, he said, some pretty good evidence that the giants also inhabited the mountains and deserts east of San Diego. As if that was not unique enough, he went on to say that a medical doctor who owned a country home east of San Diego had seen several of the creatures.

The final statement in Joel's letter was the most startling of all. He stated that the footprints he had seen were odd shaped things with four toes and a pointed heel!

Bill Early, Bud Clever and I lost no time in getting to San Diego where we met Joel and proceeded to the doctor's ranch. Joel proved to be a serious, likable and articulate young man. He told of his investigations in the regions between the coast and the Mojave Desert. He related stories of "monsters" told him by ranchers in Japatul Valley. More recent stories told of "apes" frightening horses (and people) near Alpine and of whole pens of wildfowl being carried off in one night, with only large, four toed tracks left as evidence.

Joel then gave us a more detailed description of the events at the doctor's ranch, cautioning us that for professional reasons the doctor wanted no publicity.

The doctor's first encounter with the "big monkeys," as he called them, had occurred some months earlier, just after he had purchased the ranch as a weekend home. He, his wife and their grown daughter had driven to the property late one night and had observed a giant, monkey-like creature eating from a fruit tree near the house.

The creature fled at the approach of the car and the doctor and his family returned to the city for the night.

The following day, the doctor returned to the property and found several large, four-toed tracks, quite broad at the forefoot and tapering to a pointed heel.

Upon our arrival at the ranch, we were surprised to note that it was situated only about one half mile from the freeway. As we drove up to the house, we met the doctor's daughter working in the garden. I noted the handle of a revolver protruding from the pocket of her work clothes. The doctor and his wife proved to be most gracious and cooperative in their detailed account of not only their original sighting, but of several subsequent visits from the giants. They stated that on one occasion they observed three of them, apparently a family group, standing near the fence line. The doctor had shortly before installed an electric fence completely around the property.

The doctor showed us around the property and proudly pointed out the large floodlights he had installed, commenting that they had not been visited by the "big monkeys" since the installation of the lights.

While searching the vicinity, I found a single impression in the soil not far from the doctor's property. It had the general shape and size reported by the doctor, but was very old and not clear enough to even attempt a cast. We spent several days in a careful search of the general vicinity and returned home convinced that the doctor and his family had seen something. Had it been Bigfoot?

A few weeks later we returned to the area with Joel and learned that he had been doing a good deal of leg work, talking to most of the ranchers over a very wide area. We were all convinced of the accuracy of the doctor's story, but were all skeptical of the footprint description. We had not yet learned of the hundreds of reports from the eastern and southeastern U.S., describing three-toed prints. There had been occasional reports of four-toed prints from the northwest, but we had simply assumed that they were made by individuals who had lost a toe through accident or that because of the apparent flexibility of Bigfoot toes, one toe sometimes did not leave an impression in the soil.

Joel remarked that he now had something that would change our minds. He took us to a ranch, about five miles from the doctor's place where he said the rancher had a single print to show us.

Just as Joel had indicated, the print, in fine dust, had been protected with a large plastic bowl. We were amazed to discover that the print clearly showed a V-shaped foot, 14 inches long, 10 inches wide across the four toes and with a very pointed heel. There was a deep, boulder-strewn canyon behind the ranch house and we spent the remainder of the day searching for additional prints, without success.

The following day Bill Early and Doctor Clever's son, Scott discovered two series of smaller, but similar prints on the bank of a nearby reservoir. The caretaker of the reservoir commented that he had frequently seen tracks of that description, but had assumed they were made by a large raccoon!

Although we did not discover any more footprints on that trip, we did camp out for several nights in various locations. One cold, moonlight night, while hiking to a stakeout location, Bill and I had a most memorable experience. We had always wondered just what our reaction might be if we were to come face to face with a Bigfoot. We were discussing that very subject as we walked down the lonely road to the outpost when we heard a brief whistle that seemed to originate from the brush nearby.

After a moment's pause, we continued on our way until Bill whispered, "There's something moving, over there in the brush!"

We both stopped and stared at the side of the road as a strangely shaped figure rose from the brush. As it rose to full height it seemed to be man-like except for a strange sloping shape from the head to its shoulders. The light-colored creature took several steps in our direction and Bill and I pulled our handguns. Mine was probably the slowest draw in history as I was fumbling with a camera and a flashlight.

As we directed our flashlights on the creature, several similar shapes appeared from the same direction and moved toward us. We were relieved, to say the least, to hear them speaking in Spanish and we realized that they were "wetbacks", caught in the act of sneaking into the U.S. illegally. Having seen our weapons, they apparently assumed we were officers and they were in the act of surrendering. The odd shape about their heads and shoulders proved to be blankets with which they were apparently protecting themselves from the cold.

Not wanting to waste good Bigfoot hunting time dealing with police problems, we just lined them up, (there proved to be a total of seven of them), pointed them toward the Mexican border and marched them off. Later, Doctor Clever and Scott reported that they were still marching along in single file when they passed our camp. It is several miles to the border from that spot and I often wonder if they marched all the way.

What the incident proved was that a large, man-like object appearing from out of the dark is frightening to say the least, even when you are about halfway expecting that very thing to happen. In recreating the scene, Bill stated that he had not retreated as fast as he had wanted to because I was stepping on his feet in my own efforts to retreat. He claims to still have a boot print on his right shin.

Joel Hurd eventually moved on to other areas in his Bigfoot search and left Bill and I to carry on the search in the southern part of the state. On several subsequent field trips we met some ranchers who had interesting things to say about the "monsters," but our Bigfoot hunting time grew more limited as the months went by. I had recently been transferred to command a large jail facility for Sheriff Pitchess and with 700 inmates and over 100 officers as my responsibility, I had little time for monster hunting.

After examining the results of my nearly twelve years of activity in Bigfoot research, I realized how little I had actually accomplished. Oh, yes, I had seen a few footprints, a couple of samples of probable Bigfoot feces and I had met a great many interesting people, some of whom had become my good friends, but I had not yet to even see one of the creatures, let alone photograph one. I had actually contributed little to the over-all solution of the mystery. It was obvious that Bigfoot hunting was of necessity a full-time occupation. Roger Patterson, by applying near full time to the project for seven years had finally had some success by obtaining his photographic evidence of Bigfoot.

In order to become a full time Sasquatch searcher, I decided to retire at the earliest reasonable opportunity. Beverly and I had already chosen the area for our retirement, her hometown of Colville, Washington.

By happy coincidence, Colville is only a few miles from Bossburg, where the great Bigfoot activity of 1969-70 took place.

When I mentioned to Bill Early that I was going to retire to devote full time to Bigfoot research, I made perhaps the only prophetic statement of my life. I commented that Bigfoot would probably start showing up there in Antelope Valley about the time I move away to the north woods. I was almost right. My retirement was set for July 1973, and in March, things began to happen in Antelope Valley, not far from my home. I picked up the local paper one day and read that the Marines claimed to have encountered an 8-foot tall hairy man while driving along a country road in the east end of Antelope Valley. I ignored the report, because I knew that the movie "Legend of Boggy Creek" was in town and it was enough to get any number of hoaxers into action. Besides, there is something about Bigfoot reports close to home that makes them difficult to believe. It is one thing to accept the idea of giant ape-men roaming the deep woods of the northwest or even the rugged badlands of the Mojave Desert, but reports from one's own backyard are a different thing, indeed.

Another Bigfoot sighting report was described in the same newspaper several weeks later. This time, still very dubious, I spent the day in the area around where the sighting had allegedly taken place. I was unable to find even a hint of a track in the sandy soil and came away even more convinced that it was all a joke.

A few days later I was contacted by Rich Grumly, president and founder of the California Bigfoot Organization, an active group of researchers headquartered in Palmdale. Rich and his people had taken the Antelope Valley sightings seriously from the beginning and had compiled an impressive array of casts of footprints and taped interviews of witnesses, many of whom had not been mentioned by the newspaper. It was all very convincing, although the tracks were not typical Bigfoot prints. They had obviously, however, been made by a bipedal creature of great weight and with a stride of 45 to 50 inches.

Throughout the spring of 1973 the sheriff's station and the C.B.O. people received many more reports of sightings in the east end of the valley. It was the most frustrating period of my life. Bigfoot-type creatures were apparently paying regular visits to the high desert just a few miles from my home and I had little time to investigate! My retirement date had been set, our home was sold and I was tying up the loose ends of my personal and business affairs, preparing to move to the Northwest.

I did accompany Rich on a couple of interviews and I spent several hours over the area in a sheriff's helicopter.

While flying over the area I noted several things that made sense. First, most of the sightings had been reported in localities where large poultry ranches were to be found. Also, most of the reports had originated within a few miles of the mouth of Big Rock Creek, the largest canyon in the portion of the valley and a logical route out of the mountains as it contained year-round water and good cover. The headwaters of Big Rock Creek are near the Devils Canyon-Bear Canyon Wild area, a remote and seldom traveled wilderness in the mountains that separate Antelope Valley from the Los Angeles Basin. I was not too surprised then to learn that the sheriff's station had received a report from 3 young men who claimed to have been followed out of Big Rock Canyon by a 9-foot-tall, slender, hair-covered man. Their story was substantiated a few days later with the discovery of 17-inch-long footprints near the campground where they had camped.

This whole situation would have been hilarious if it had not been so frustrating. I had spent every spare moment for a dozen years, poking around in California and Nevada in search of the elusive giants. Now I found myself making preparations to move away from the area of greatest Bigfoot activity in the world at the time. As of the time of this writing, at least two research groups are still working in Antelope Valley.

The Search, Present and Future

My ol' fishin' buddy, Bob Hewes, and I have now organized the Sasquatch Investigation Council, headquartered here in Colville. It's made up of local businessmen and Bigfoot buffs, and is one of the best-equipped groups in the country. We have available to us several airplanes, snowmobiles, a tranquilizer gun and considerable photographic equipment. Our time has so far been spent primarily in researching the Bigfoot record for northeast Washington, and it appears that the creatures make fairly frequent appearances hereabouts, or at least have in years past.

My home is just over the hill from Bossburg where more than a thousand tracks were found in 1969. So, now... if only Bigfoot will just cooperate.

Chapter 3
The Mystery Grows

As indicated in the first two chapters, the history of the Bigfoot phenomenon, or rather, the history of modern man's reaction to it has fallen into three fairly distinct phases.

First was that period prior to the Bluff Creek excitement of 1958. For many years, people had been trying to report their encounters with the creatures, but with little success—or at best, with only local success.

After 1958, a number of amateur researchers got involved in more-or-less individual and unrelated efforts directed toward solving the mystery. That second period lasted roughly ten years.

By the late 1960s, the third phase had arrived. Newspapers and magazines were reporting Sasquatch stories, and investigations by amateurs continued, only this time, they established communication links between one another.

The fourth phase was expected at any time, and we

all assumed it would include the capture of a Bigfoot. We assumed this would confirm our speculations about the giant apeman. It would vindicate us. Unfortunately Bigfoot has yet to be caught.

In my opinion, the fourth phase is now upon us and it includes, among other things, the realization that we are dealing with not one, but several distinct types of giants. Some of our latest findings now hint at things that can only be described as mind bending!

All We Need Is A Specimen?

In the spring of 1968, most of the active Bigfoot researchers in the country gathered in Willow Creek, California for a showing of the Patterson film. Among those present were George Haas, John Dana, John Green, Jim Mcclarin and Syl McCoy. A meeting was held afterwards at Syl's home to discuss the film. Taking what we had seen in the film and combining it with information gleaned from the many reports we had received, we drew up a composite word-picture of the elusive giants we had all been pursuing.

Physical Description:

Bigfoot is a massive bipedal hair-covered creature, almost certainly a primate. It has some over-all similarities to man in bodily proportions, but with slightly longer arms and shorter legs and little or no neck. The size for adult specimens ranges from 7 to 10 feet in height; the estimated weight ranges from 600 to 1000 pounds. The hair coloring variations are similar to that of other primates, ranging from reddish-brown through brown, yellow brown, black, grey, silver-tipped and white.

The facial and head characteristics are similar to

the gorilla, with a sharply slanting forehead. No external ears are in evidence, but possibly hidden by hair. It has a massive jaw and flat nose. The eyes are small, round, set deeply under heavy brow ridges and are most commonly recorded as bright glowing red.

Our sitings indicate that they walk on the soles of their feet somewhat similar to man's but with no arch. There is a somewhat greater uniformity of toe size than in man and the toes are possibly webbed.

Other descriptions we arrived at included Bigfoot's powerful stench and high-pitched, whistling scream.

Diet:

We determined that it ate primarily vegetable matter with some fish and even garbage, when available.

Habits:

It is apparently shy, retiring and nocturnal, and generally travels alone, although a few reports mention pairs or family groups.

Habitat:

Generally the heavily forested mountain country of the Pacific Northwest seems to be the most likely environment. A few reports have come from desert areas, but it is assumed that, most likely, the creatures were en-route from one mountainous region to another.

It also seemed reasonable to assume that Bigfoot was simply a very primitive man-like primate that had somehow become lost in the evolutionary shuffle. He had probably arrived in North America the same way the Indians had, from Siberia, over the land bridge to Alaska. Bigfoot had probably arrived before the first Indians, but after their arrival, it had been driven into the mountains and with the coming of the White Man had retreated even further.

We also know that the North American Bigfoot had near relatives in other parts of the world—the Yeti of the Himalayas.

So we knew what Bigfoot looked like, what he ate, where he had come from and where he ranged. All we needed to bring this matter to a proper conclusion was a specimen in the flesh—dead or alive... or so we thought. As a matter of fact, we had only scratched the surface of a mystery that, to this day, becomes ever more baffling.

A Second Look

Along about 1970, I, for one, was becoming more than a little disturbed by the many extreme variations in the Bigfoot theme. In the spring of 1970 I prepared a paper for circulation among Bigfoot researchers pointing to the possibility that the giants inhabit not only the Northwest forests, but also the deserts and mountains of Southern California, including some of the mountains of Los Angeles County. Most of the other Sasquatchers were polite enough to comment favorably upon the paper, but in truth, I believe they found the idea a bit too much to accept.

It was only a few months after completion of my paper that I was contacted by Joel Hurd with information about the four-toed tracks near San Diego. Something had made those big V-shaped tracks and that "something" had been described by eye-witnesses as a creature very similar to old Bigfoot of the Northwest.

Those San Diego County tracks disturbed me more than a little. Despite the descriptions of the creatures themselves, the tracks were so totally different than "typical" Bigfoot tracks that they must have been made by a creature of at least a different species. A foot of that shape would appear to be totally non-functional for use by a heavy-bodied, bipedal primate. It would be logical for a greatly, oversize duck perhaps—but a primate with four toes and a very pointed heel?

Using more than a little imagination, I was able to develop a theory to explain those odd-shaped tracks.

To begin with, Eastern San Diego County is separated from the desert by a narrow range of mountains. That low desert area was, until a few hundred years ago, a vast series of lakes that became swampy marshlands as they evaporated. Marks of the ancient water level can still be seen on many of the desert rocks.

I theorized that a geographical sub-group of Sasquatch-type creatures had, through many thousands of years, evolved a foot shape efficient for slogging around in the muddy swamplands. Now, with the lakes gone, that foot shape is still quite efficient for use on the sandy desert floor. With the luxuriant flora and fauna of the swamplands long gone, the few remaining apemen found it necessary to range far and wide for sustenance. What more logical place to search for food than the poultry and cattle ranches of the sparsely-settled area of nearby Eastern San Diego County?

Up to that particular point in time, we had not really been successful in convincing the public that a race of hairy giants were roaming the forest of the Northwest. We had not even tried to sell the idea of the "little people," the small, hairy man-like creatures occasionally reported from the bayou country and from a few places in the Northwest. As John Green had said, "lets just deal with one mystery at a time."

Fine. But what about this, Southern California evidence that indicates there are hairy giants in that arid country that are similar to, but possibly not quite the same, as Bigfoot of the Northwest?

As mentioned previously, the area from which Bigfoot reports originate seems to grow in direct proportion to the spread of investigators activities. By the early 1970s, it began to appear as if almost any area of North America could be considered Bigfoot range if there was an investigator there to dig up the information. That was easy enough to accept as long as the reports came from such places as Michigan and Wisconsin, with vast forest areas. Despite the occasional reports from Nevada and Southern California, we were still thinking of the giants as residents of the mountains and forests of the North. Then we heard that the Navajos of Northern New Mexico were complaining about the upright walking "bears" that had been stealing sheep.

From the Southeast, we heard that a somewhat shorter, stockier Bigfoot-like creature was occasionally seen in certain swampy areas of Florida, where he was called "Skunk-Ape."

Our neat little picture of Bigfoot as a creature of the Northwest woods was beginning to crumble. We were not surprised then to learn of "The Legend of Boggy Creek," a semi-documentary film based on reports of a hairy monster occasionally seen in and around the swampy areas of Foulke, Arkansas. The film was well done and truly believable except for one thing.

I commented that, "It was a shame they had to hoke it up with that silly looking three-toed track in one scene."

The creature appeared to be no more than a southern version of the Northwest Sasquatch and it seemed that they could have come up with a better and more believable footprint, real or fabricated.

My comments relative to the Boggy Creek prints were to appear a bit silly when, a short time later the results of the work of investigator Loren Coleman began to reach us. Loren pointed out that the majority of tracks from the Southeastern and Eastern United States were shaped somewhat like swim-fins and with just three toes. If this had been just a local phenomenon, it could have been passed off as a hoax, but Coleman reported tracks of that description from Missouri, Indiana and Wisconsin in addition to the Arkansas reports.

Obviously then, our understanding of Bigfoot as an unknown species of ape-men who had somehow survived in a few isolated mountain areas of the Northwest was a theory badly in need of revision. Ape-men of various sizes and shapes were, by that time, being reported from nearly every region of the U.S., Western Canada, and even Northern Mexico. To make matters worse, the distinct variations in foot shape, alone, were sufficient to make it appear that North America is inhabited by at least four species, races, types or whatever, of hairy *hominids* presently unknown to science.

Anthropologists had been less than receptive to the original Sasquatch concept, so we well-knew they were going to be downright hysterical when we tried to convince them of the validity of our latest findings—but the worst was yet to come!

I undertook the task of re-checking the files to see just how many atypical reports had been ignored by the Bigfoot researchers through the years. I was surprised and a bit embarrassed to learn that a small, but definite, percentage of the reports from the beginning had not fit the "accepted" Bigfoot data... literally from the beginning. The earliest Bigfoot report by a White Man that we have discovered is the David Thompson narrative of 1811 that had described four-toed tracks.

In 1960, Bud Ryerson reported 16-inch-long four-toed tracks crossing a logging road near Weitchpec in Northern California. Similar tracks were found in Shasta County, California on January 6, 1971.

The tracks reported in conjunction with a sighting near Dixie, Idaho in September 1972 were described as having four toes and a four-foot stride.

It is accepted as fact among police investigators that no two eye-witnesses will describe the same person or crime scene in exactly the same way. Sometimes the discrepancies are so great as to thoroughly confuse an otherwise clear picture of a crime. I have known three witnesses with good eyesight to report three totally different colors when describing a getaway car. It is not surprising, then, to find that shocked and frightened Bigfoot observers often do not agree exactly as to what they saw.

Even taking into consideration the well-known lack of eye-witness reliability, the files disclosed certain discrepancies that occurred often enough to be significant. For instance, we know that Northwest Bigfoot reports describe a massive, heavy-bodied creature with relatively long arms and short legs. The head, as in the Patterson film, is large, even taking into consideration the size of the torso. However, a certain number of reports through the years have described giants with long legs. A small head is sometimes described and it would be difficult for a witness, even an excited one, to see the Patterson Sasquatch as a creature with a small head.

From time to time, someone describes a tall, slender ape-man. At first thought, one might assume such reports concern individuals that vary slightly from the normal, as in any other species. However, sketches drawn by the witnesses in some cases display a genuinely slender creature, which differs greatly from our incidents of information.

There were also some notable differences in reported reflective eye color. Red and orange were most common, but green, clear, yellow-green and yellow had also been reported. Interestingly, some night-time reports had failed to mention any eye reflection at all, even while a light was shining on the creature.

By 1972, it was beginning to dawn on some of the more dedicated Sasquatchers that our picture of a "typical" Bigfoot was unsuited to a surprising proportion of the reports then coming to our attention.

The Antelope Valley "Creatures"

As described in Chapter 2, the spring of 1973 produced a number of sightings and tracks not far from my home in Northern Los Angeles County. By that point in time, I should not have been too surprised to learn of the Antelope Valley sightings. In my paper on the subject, I had described nearly a dozen cases of Bigfoot evidence in the mountains and deserts of Southern California. As far back as 1969, I had heard the teenagers talk of the "Rag Man" or "Mummy Man" of the Palmdale Hills. Because of the name, I had assumed that they were talking about some poor beggar or hermit who lived in the hills. As it turned out, the Rag Man was a big, hairy man-thing that had been seen in the hills near Palmdale. It had eventually become quite an exciting pastime for the teenagers to go into the hills at night and frighten themselves silly looking for the Rag Man. It was not until the 1973 events became common knowledge that I learned what they had been up to.

At first the Palmdale sightings seemed normal enough. First, three Marines reported to the sheriff that they had seen a dark, 8-foot, hairy man alongside the road at 110th and Avenue J at 1:00 a.m. on March 14th. Ten days later, 19-year old Kim McDonald reported a hairy giant in her yard, just a mile from the location of the sighting by the Marines.

Miss McDonald's interview was one of the most convincing I have heard. She stated that she came home from a babysitting job at 2:30 a.m. on a moonlight night. As she walked from her car to the house, she observed a 7-foot-tall, hairy creature rise from the alfalfa field nearby and run off on two legs. The McDonald's dog was found injured the next day and sometime later was found dead, with its legs pulled from its body.

Sixteen-year-old Jim Parkhurst of Lancaster reported that at 10:45 a.m. on April 14th, about two miles west of the McDonald's residence, that he had seen an ape-man run across the road. Parkhurst had been driving east at the time, in broad daylight, in good weather. He stated to me that he had the creature in clear view for about 5 or 6 seconds as it loped across the road about one quarter mile in front of his car. He particularly noted that the upper body was bent slightly and that the arms had displayed considerable swinging motion. He said the creature was about 7-feet-tall, black, and with a "more or less round head that was kind of small."

Young Parkhurst then made one comment that may or may not be significant in the light of subsequent events. I asked him what happened to the creature after it crossed the road. He answered that it ran on into the desert and disappeared. I went to the location the next day and was disturbed by the "just disappeared" statement. The area is one of low sand dunes, too soft for good footprints, and there were some very low shrubbery and a few joshua trees. There was also a very slight depression that is, in reality, a small, dry wash, but hardly sufficient to hide a 7-foot monster in broad daylight. Keep in mind, also, that Parkhurst's vehicle reached the spot where the giant had crossed the road only seconds after the beast had entered the desert. At the time, I had some doubts about the story because of the rapid disappearance of the creature. Today I am not so sure.

To that point, the sightings had seemed typical enough except for the lack of information about odor or eye reflection. Of course, two of the sightings had been made from vehicles and Miss McDonald had been too frightened to remember many details. Rich Grumley's C.B.O. people were doing most of the follow-up on the Antelope Valley information and Rich told me that he had found several large five-toed prints near the McDonald ranch. I was more than a little startled when I saw some photos and casts of those footprints. The tracks had five toes all right, but the over-all shape and proportions of the 14-inch prints were unlike any I had ever seen—that is, with one exception. On pages 40 and 41 of Green's *Year of The Sasquatch* is something similar, but it is purportedly the print of a mythical species, an Asian version of our Bigfoot. Things were beginning to get complicated, but there were many more surprises to come.

58

I have before me a copy of a Los Angeles County Sheriff's Department memorandum dated April 17, 1973, titled "Possible Bigfoot Sighting." It states that at 0005 hours, William Roemerman, 16; Richard Engels, 15; and Brian Gooloojarb, 17 arrived at the Antelope Valley Station to make the following report:

While driving down Big Rock Creek Road in their pickup truck they had been followed for a short time by a 10-foot-tall, slender, two-legged creature covered with hair. Roemerman and Engels were riding in the bed of the truck and as the driver pulled over and slowed to allow another vehicle to pass, the monster-man had run out into the road and loped along behind the truck for about ten seconds.

It was several weeks before I had an opportunity to interview any of the boys and by then they had made several return trips to the scene in daylight. On their first return trip they had found and cast a number of 17-inch-long three-toed footprints. Things were beginning to get a bit out of hand by that time in Southern California, with a total now of four different types of tracks, and three of them from the Antelope Valley. Of course, the boys could have been faking the whole thing, but as the reader will learn as we go along, subsequent events in Antelope Valley make that seem most unlikely.

The UFO-ologists

From time to time through the years, the suggestion had been made that there might be a connection between the two great mysteries of our time, Bigfoot and UFOs. All serious Bigfoot researchers rejected that idea totally. The UFOs represent a most advanced technology, Bigfoot on the other hand is obviously at the opposite end of evolutionary beings. It seemed like a most preposterous suggestion. Perhaps it is just that, but some interesting events have occurred in the last two years that have caused some of us to wonder.

I had simply ignored the suggestion of the UFO connection even after I had received an unusual report from investigator Mike Bershod of Baltimore, Maryland. In a letter describing his investigation of the "Sykesville Monster" that had been frequently reported around Sykesville, Maryland, in 1973, he made a casual reference to an unusual facet of the investigation. He had learned that the day before the monster sightings had begun, an anonymous caller had reported to the police that a UFO had been seen lowering a dark object into the woods near where the sightings later occurred. Mike obviously did not place any great credence in the story and neither did I, at the time.

Just a week later, I first heard from Ann Slate. She called, explaining that she had come across my name while investigating the Antelope Valley sightings for an article she was writing. She went on to explain that she was really a UFO buff, but like many UFO investigators, had begun to suspect that the two phenomena were actually part of the same mystery. Shortly thereafter, she sent me some of the results of her own studies that tended to support her theories somewhat. I was certainly not convinced, nor were any of the Sasquatchers that I passed it on to. Then Stan Gordon's MUFON report came in from Pennsylvania and it was a shocker!

Pennsylvania 1973, Bigfoot?

The report referred to above is the 21-page paper that Stan Gordon submitted to the 1974 MUFON, UFO symposium. Gordon, at age 25, is one of the youngest state directors in the MUFON (Mutual UFO Network) organization. He was also founder and director of the Westmoreland County Pennsylvania UFO study group, which is established as a statewide clearinghouse and is staffed by specialized individuals, including scientists and engineers. The fact that the local police so quickly called upon Gordon and his people for assistance in the matter is clear evidence of the respect they have for his organization, even though there was no indication of UFO activity in the first reports.

Gordon appeared to be a most careful and methodical investigator and, of equal importance here, he was in the right place at the right time. Between June 1973 and February 1974, a total of 118 "ape-man" sightings were reported in Pennsylvania; the majority of them from Westmoreland County. Stan found himself, therefore, in the very center of the greatest concentration of sightings in history and he had a well-staffed and equipped organization to conduct the necessary investigation.

Keep in mind if you will, that, as bizarre as some of these alleged sightings may seem, they appear to have been as carefully investigated and recorded as any in Sasquatchery.

Except for the fact that it had occurred in Pennsylvania, the first incident seemed believable enough. A man living on Rodabaugh Road, Greengate, just off Rt. 30 had noticed a foul odor while shaving late the previous night. It was a warm July night and he had left the window open. The rotten cucumber-odor seemed to be coming through the window. As he turned to close the window, he looked into a pair of glowing red eyes peering at him through the window. Other members of the family smelled the rotten odor and they also noticed at the time that their usually noisy dogs had not uttered a sound all evening.

During his investigation of the incident, Gordon learned from the witness' 14-year-old son that he and some friends had recently seen a tall, gorilla-like creature in a nearby wooded area. Gordon accompanied the boys to the spot and found a perfect 13-inch by 8-inch three-toed footprint. Although he found only one clear print, other nearby areas in the immediate vicinity appeared to have been walked upon by a heavy creature.

That same day, Gordon received a message that a similar report had come from New Sewickley Township, about 50 miles away. Gordon knew he was on to something and released the information to the news media, hoping that other witnesses would come forward. Within hours, his control board and local police agencies were flooded with telephone calls.

Another result of the publicity was that the wooded areas of Westmoreland and surrounding counties in Pennsylvania had suddenly become over-run with heavily armed monster hunters and a great many sightings were claimed.

The locality that appeared to be the center of greatest activity was the heavily-wooded area between Latrobe and Derry in Westmoreland County. Many witnesses there reported face-to-face encounters with the giants. The Chief of Police of Derry asked Gordon to investigate a monster supposedly sighted by a woman and her daughter at 2:30 a.m. on August 21. That sighting is particularly interesting because of the facial details described by the witness. The woman, lying in bed and unable to sleep due to the August heat, looked up from the bed to see an ape-like face peering at her through the window. Too frightened to cry out, the witness simply stared back at the monster.

She described the creature's eyes as "upright and oval," dark with no whites, and with no lids or lashes. The nose was "pushed-in." When she finally recovered sufficiently to move, the creature backed away from the window and walked to the front of the house where it was observed by the witness' daughter. They also reported that for days their house smelled of rotten meat.

During the next week, a number of similar reports were received from Youngstown, Herminie and Whitney, Pennsylvania. The creatures frequently were reported in residential areas, snooping about in yards and even in trailer courts. They seemed particularly interested houses containing young children.

Mr. Chester Yothers of Whitney called the state police at 4:30 a.m. to report an 8-foot-tall, hairy man-like creature in his yard. Six state police troopers arrived at the scene to find a series of fresh footprints in the dew. A neighbor living three doors away reported that, at about the same time, she had seen a tall, dark figure in the driveway behind the Yother residence. She stated that she had detected a strong sulphur odor at the time. The state police called Gordon to investigate. The Yothers' were so frightened by the experience that they left home and did not return for a week.

Gordon is, of course, a UFO buff first and he commented that there had been a rash of UFO sightings over Pennsylvania during the same period of time as the incidents above described. On October 25, an event was reported that seemed to show a more definite relationship between UFO and the Bigfoot-like creatures.

At 10:30 p.m. on that date, the state police at Uniontown called MUFON headquarters seeking their aid to investigate a report of a sighting that included both hairy giants and an apparent UFO. The witness stated that, about 9:00 p.m., he and 14 other persons had seen a large, red, glowing ball descend toward a pasture on his farm. The witness ran to his house to get his 30.06 rifle and then he and two neighbor boys jumped into his pickup truck and headed for the pasture. As they approached the pasture, the electrical system of the truck failed, so they parked the truck and walked on up the hill.

They observed a bright white, metallic, circular object resting on the ground. They estimated its size at about 100-feet in diameter. One of the boys then pointed out 2 tall ape-like creatures with green-glowing eyes nearby. The creatures were making a crying sound and there was an odor of burning rubber in the air. The creatures were approaching the witnesses, so one of the witnesses fired a shot over the ape-men's heads. When that did not stop them, he fired three shots directly into the body of the first one. It stopped, raised its hand and the UFO "just disappeared." The creatures then slowly turned and lumbered into the woods.

This science-fiction-type story could be easily put aside as a hoax except for the following additional circumstances. Gordon quotes the state trooper as reporting that when he arrived at the scene, he observed a glowing white illuminated area about 100 feet in diameter at the point where the witnesses claimed the UFO had landed. He further stated that the illuminated area was almost bright enough to read a newspaper. His attempts to investigate the area were interfered with by the fact that one witness was near hysteria. The trooper and witnesses then returned to the police barracks and Gordon was called.

Gordon, accompanied by his assistants, George Lutz, a retired Air Force major; Dave Smith, a physics instructor; Dennis Smeltzer, a sociology major; and Dave Burke, a professional photographer, rushed to the scene. In company with a witness, they searched the area thoroughly. The glowing ring of light was no longer visible, but it was observed that the farm animals would not enter that area of the field. A radiation check of the spot proved negative. They then observed that the farm animals apparently had been frightened by something farther up in the field. As the investigators and the witness walked toward that portion of the field, the witness and two of Gordon's men began acting strangely. The witness collapsed, knocking Lutz to the ground with him, then Smeltzer complained of dizziness and fell to his knees. They all noticed a sulphur-like odor in the air. Gordon then quickly directed his men and the witness from the scene.

Just one week later, the chief of police of Midland, Beaver County, reported sighting a large disc-shaped object hovering over the towns of Industry and Ohioville. The police of those towns were at that very time investigating reports of a "strange animal" prowling about. The following morning a trail of 11-inch-long, three-toed footprints was found.

A short time later, a woman living near Uniontown reported to police that she had fired a shotgun blast into the body of a giant ape-man she had caught prowling in her yard. She stated that as she fired, "there was a flash of light and the thing just disappeared."

A number of other incidents were reported to Gordon in which the ape-men, when shot—and, in one case, when struck by a car—literally vanished in a flash of light.

To further complicate the situation, as if it needed

any further complication, is the fact that there were apparently several different types of creatures involved in the Pennsylvania incidents.

The majority of reports seem, at first, to describe our good old "typical" Northwest Sasquatch—a 7- or 8-foot bipedal creature with an ape-like face. The eyes are described as about the size of golfballs and glowing bright red, green or white. However, other characteristics differ considerably from most sighting reports of the Northwest creatures. For instance, the long arms—in some cases nearly touching the ground—visible ears, and prominent fangs are non-existent in typical Bigfoot reports. The frequently-reported sound, as that of a baby crying, was another unusual feature of the Pennsylvania reports.

Several of the reports described a creature 5- or 6-feet-tall, somewhat more man-like except for the hair covering, and the extremely long arms. In each case where these particular creatures were reported, their apparent agility was commented upon and odor was never mentioned.

There were also several reports of smaller, monkey-like creatures. I have heard from another source that primate-like tracks were discovered on several occasions, but that in all cases, the toes appeared to be shorter than in any known species.

As if all that is not sufficiently bizarre, several reports describe a creature about the size of a large dog, with a long, ringed tail and large red eyes.

It is admittedly an awfully big jump from giant man-like footprints on a logging road in the Northwest to UFO-borne ape-men in Pennsylvania—ape-men that appear to have the ability to disappear in a flash of light. Because our investigation concerns itself with the mysterious hair-covered man-like giants of North America, we cannot totally ignore these Pennsylvania sightings simply because the reports contain certain elements we find terribly difficult to accept. To begin with, as previously mentioned, Gordon reports 118 sighting incidents in an 8-month period in the state of Pennsylvania; 91 of them in Westmorland County. To clarify, he had 118 sightings after eliminating all obvious hoaxes and publicity-seeking tricks. Those 118 sightings produced 245 witnesses, by far the largest concentration of "Bigfoot" activity ever reported.

In attempting to pass judgement on these astounding reports the reader should ask himself if it is likely that a total of 245 citizens of all ages, from throughout the state, would likely cooperate in the perpetration of a great hoax. It also should be pointed out here that Gordon and the police measured, cast and photographed many hundreds of footprints and also collected several fecal and hair samples.

And what of Gordon himself? Could the whole thing be the figment of his imagination? Certainly not, there are simply too many people to back his story. Gordon is well-respected in his field, frequently lectures to professional and civic organizations and has appeared on a number of radio and television shows. Added to that is the fact that Gordon's group is not alone in its investigations of the Pennsylvania incidents. In addition to the various police agencies involved, an organization known as SITU was active in Westmoreland County at the time. SITU (Society for Investigation of the Unexplained) was organized by the widow of Ivan Sanderson of "Abominable Snowman fame." The SITU people came up with evidence fully-supporting that reported by Gordon.

It would be easiest, of course, to just ignore the whole Pennsylvania business and hope it will go away. Unfortunately, things keep happening in various parts of the country that seem to be related to that unbelievable situation.

I have before me a letter on U.S. Department of Interior stationary describing certain strange incidents that have occurred on an Indian reservation. The letter was written to me by an official of the Department of Interior, Bureau of Indian Affairs. For obvious reasons I cannot give the man's name, nor can I identify the reservation.

This man, a 20-year veteran of the Indian Service states "I have not been too involved in Sasquatch research on the reservation, primarily because our UFO situation has assumed such a scope as to take up all my spare time. Although, in my opinion, and the opinion of many others, the two things tie together. I feel they must be researched separately."

Meanwhile, during the time that the incredible Pennsylvania monster flap was in progress, hairy giants were showing up in other widely-separated parts of the country. One of the most publicized was the so-called "Murphysboro Monster;" the slimy, foul-smelling 8-foot creature that walked up out of the Big Muddy River and frightened the daylights out of local residents. That story began about midnight, June 28. Randy Needham and Judy Johnson were in a car parked down by the river. They heard a high-pitched shriek from the nearby woods. They then observed a light-colored, hairy, 8-foot-tall man-like thing, covered with river slime. Needham and his girlfriend drove hurriedly from the scene and straight to the police headquarters to report the incident.

Police Officer Jimmie Nash and Deputy Sheriff Bob Scott proceeded to the scene, found some odd-looking three-toed tracks and, while inspecting them, were startled by a scream described as a greatly amplified eagle shriek.

The following night, Randy Creath and Cheryl Ray were sitting on her front porch when they heard something moving in the nearby bushes. Cheryl went to turn on a yard-light and Randy went to investigate. At that moment an "8-foot tall, white gorilla" stepped from the bushes. The teenagers and the beast stared at each other for a few seconds before the monster turned and crashed off through the brush, back toward the river.

Several similar incidents were reported to the police during the next few days. Chief of Police, Toby Berger, commented that he believed the witnesses' statements and he put his entire 14-man force on the alert for the creature. On one occasion, a tracking dog followed the scent to an abandoned barn, but when heavily-armed officers kicked-in the door, the barn was empty.

According to researcher Ann Slate, the towns of Charleston, Scott City, Pevely, Crystal City and Danby, Illinois produced reports of low flying UFOs during that same period. Those towns are all within a 70-mile radius of Murphysboro.

Several Bigfoot-type incidents were reported from the southern states during the same period, perhaps the most interesting from Hollywood, Florida. Richard Lee Smith, who lived at 1701 State Road 27, Hollywood, called the highway patrol and stated that he had hit a "two-legged gorilla." He reported that the incident had occurred on State Road 27, near Kroma Avenue, and that after being hit, the creature ran off into the brush.

One newspaper report of the incident stated that Patrolman Robert Holmeyer of the Hialeah Gardens Police Department also saw the creature at a distance. He said it "looked like an extremely large man, about 8-feet."

By spring 1974, Ann Slate had become actively involved in the Antelope Valley, California, area where monster activity was still being reported. I had always wondered about the three-toed tracks supposedly found by the teenagers in Big Rock Creek the previous spring. At the time, I had not heard of any other three-toed tracks west of the Rockies. Then in the summer of 1974, Ann Slate and her group found three-toed prints at Sycamore Flats Campground in Big Rock Creek, near the spot where Richard Engels and his companions had reported the 10-foot-tall, slender giant. That location, by the way, is in the same range of foothills, just a few miles east of the reported sightings of the "Rag Man of Palmdale."

During the same period of time, additional reports of three-toed tracks came from various points in the far west. A man and his son claimed to have found 20-inch, three-toed tracks in hard-packed gravel in Northeastern Oregon, near Enterprise. At about the same time, there was another unconfirmed report of three-toed tracks from somewhere in the Sierras.

In October, Mrs. Slate reported that she and her husband had found a series of 15-inch three-toed tracks at Black Butte, in the eastern end of Antelope Valley. Ranchers had reported noticing an eerie silence all summer in that high desert area. No coyotes howling and very little sign of wildlife, anywhere.

An interesting question arises at this point. Were the three-toed creatures there all along?... and had we just not seen their tracks? Or were they something new to the area?

The following report from Antelope Valley is the only one so far recorded wherein eye reflection is mentioned, and it is a bit of a surprise. Information has been received that the Air Police at Edwards Air Base, a huge rocket fuel testing complex near Palmdale, had reported encounters with hairy giants. We have been able to confirm only one of those sightings. A Sergeant House of the Air Police reported that in checking the desert area with his spotlight, the beam had picked up two bright blue "lights" at a distance of about 200 yards. As the bright objects moved toward him, he realized they were the eyes of a very large creature that crouched in the brush, watching him. Because of the brush, he was never able to get a clear view of the creature. The sergeant then received a call that required his services in another part of the base. When he returned several hours later, he found nothing.

We have reason to believe that a number of other Air Police on the base have information related to sightings, but are reluctant to talk—either for fear of ridicule or possibly on orders from their superiors.

The latest information from Southern California concerns a group of researchers who investigated reports of a Bigfoot in the San Gabriel Mountains a few miles north of Pasadena. The group backpacked into the area, down a narrow mountain trail, late in the afternoon. After setting up camp and readying their infra-red photo equipment, they climbed into their sleeping bags as protection against the chill of the November night. Shortly thereafter, their camp was bombarded by huge rocks, thrown from the trail above their camp. The rocks, far too large to have been thrown by a human, seemed to be aimed to narrowly miss the frightened investigators. After a few minutes, the bombardment stopped, to be repeated a half dozen times before dawn. On two occasions a deep-throated bellow was heard coming from the same direction as the rocks.

The sound was described by one investigator as similar to the roar of a bull elephant, but louder!

The investigators never saw the rock-thrower and left hurriedly the next day without finding any tracks. It is my understanding that this particular group has given up its night stakeouts.

And next?

We have come a long way since Bluff Creek, 1958. In those 16 years, we have, to a degree, "solved" the Bigfoot mystery. We now have a fairly complete file on those creatures of the Northwest, and we pretty well understand what it is we are looking for. In addition, we find ourselves in a seemingly ever-expanding series of weird phenomena. The reports of giant ape-men, once thought to be purely a product of the northwestern forests, now originate from nearly every state in the union. To the names Sasquatch, Bigfoot and Oh-Ma of the Northwest, we must add the Skunk Ape of Florida, Mo-Mo the Missouri Monster, the Murphysboro Monster, the Legend of Boggy Creek, the Borrego Sandman and many others.

What does it all mean? In a later chapter I will attempt to analyze and summarize the evidence so that the reader can draw his own conclusions. My only comment at this point is that it is obvious that a lot of funny-looking things are wandering around in the forests, deserts, bayous and other out-of-the-way places in this country. Also, it appears that some of them just might be—well—from out of this world.

Chapter 4
Hoax, Hysteria & Mis-identification

*Y*ou'll never get me to believe those stories about giant
ape-men roaming through the forests of North America!

Such skepticism is the usual reaction of most people
upon hearing of Bigfoot for the first time. The listener's
initial conclusion being that the story is fabricated in its
entirety.

*Here in 20th century America, all species of
indigenous wildlife have been classified and catalogued.
How could one of the very largest creatures on the
continent have gone undetected, and a primate at that?*

Most any determined skeptic can construct what
appears to be a good case against the possible existence of
ape-men in North America. It can be argued that if ape-
men did inhabit this continent, there would surely be at
least a few specimens in zoos or in museum collections.
It can also be pointed out that not even one specimen has
been brought in. Last, but not least, we can be reminded

that hoaxers have fooled a good many people with fake tracks in the snow.

Upon being confronted with the evidence, both physical and eye-witness, the skeptic will explain it all away as either,(a) hoax, (b) mass hysteria, (c) mistaken identity.

I have heard each of these theories advanced at one time or another. Perhaps we should more closely examine the "explanations" that are so readily acceptable to the confirmed skeptic.

The Hoax

For years, our answer to the hoax theory was that never has any Bigfoot evidence been proven fake. No one had ever been caught in the act of faking tracks and not one set of false feet had ever been found. But, as might be expected, the pranksters have finally gotten into the act. A local citizen of Arden, Washington, claimed to have used false feet to create footprints near Arden in the early part of 1970. No doubt other hoaxers have been at work in one place or another, but hardly in sufficient numbers to support the hoax theory.

There are two reasons to reject the hoax theory. (a) It would take a gigantic, world-wide organization to pull it off; (b) it would have to be a co-ordinated effort, which seems unlikely.

The only point that tends to support the idea of a single great conspiracy is the amazing similarity between footprints found in various areas of the country. Even though there are several different types of tracks popping up in North America, there is a certain definite consistency as to the details within each type. That fact is one of the strongest arguments to support the validity of the footprints.

To believe that hundreds of individuals are working in unison to perpetuate this fraud world wide is an impossibility.

A detailed analysis of the prints will be found in a later chapter. A close study of the footprint evidence alone is usually sufficient to convince most interested people of the genuine nature of the Bigfoot mystery. When we take into account the sightings of hairy giants so frequently reported in conjunction with the discovery of footprints, the entire hoax theory becomes ridiculous.

As a further argument to destroy the hoax idea, we can consider the obvious weight of whatever or whoever is making the tracks. The prints are invariably impressed into the soil to a depth that could only be accomplished by an ape-man weighing hundreds of pounds more than a large human. For the hoaxer to create such tracks would almost certainly require the design, construction and use of a most remarkable machine.

That marvel would necessarily stamp the prints into the soil, but the prints do not show any evidence of stamping. The machine would also be required to stride along on two "legs," step over logs, climb and descend steep banks and negotiate rivers and lakes.

The most remarkable thing about this imaginary device would have to be the fact that it was obviously designed many years ago and would have had to be a tremendously advanced piece of engineering. Also, we must assume that some method has been devised to enable its operators to transport it into dozens of localities without attracting attention.

If the idea of such a fantastic machine is a little far-fetched for your imagination, then we can consider the possibility that the organization that is conspiring to create the great hoax has sent a number of workers into the woods to make the tracks by hand. Of course, we are still faced with the problem of the depth of the prints, the stride and the apparent superhuman strength and agility of the print-maker.

To be expected to believe that such an organization has been in operation these many years is certainly a test of one's credulity. How could the organization have existed all this time, operating throughout the world without anyone even hinting of it? I have never heard or seen anything that would lead one to believe that there is such an organization.

The Lie-Detector

It has been suggested time and again that the polygraph or "lie-detector" should be used in our investigations to determine the honesty of alleged witnesses. Although it may seem like a sound idea, it is based upon some misconceptions concerning the polygraph.

The primary purpose of the polygraph is to determine whether or not the subject has guilty knowledge of the crime. So, presumably, a hoaxer might well be exposed if he was willing to undergo polygraph examination. If, on the other hand, he is psychotic and believes his own story, then the lie detector would prove nothing. The same would be true in the case where the witness had made an honest mistake as to the identity of the beast and had, in good faith, reported a Sasquatch sighting.

There are a number of other drawbacks to the use of

the polygraph that tend to make it a less than desirable tool in Sasquatch investigation. First of all, its use requires the services of a trained operator, making it an expensive proposition. Also, many witnesses might well be offended at having their honesty questioned. That, of course, would leave considerable doubt as to the reason for the refusal. Did the witness refuse to submit to the test because he had, in fact, lied, or was it because he was angry at having his honesty questioned?

One of the few cases in which the polygraph was used was the 1965 Frenchtown, Michigan, episode. In that case, two sets of tests were administered with apparently conflicting results. The persons involved were Mrs. George Bush, her daughter, Mrs. Ruth Owens and 17-year old Christine Van Acker.

It was a warm night and the three women were driving along a country road in a wooded area. Christine was driving and the vehicle windows were open. Mrs. Owens sighted something ahead and yelled at Christine. Christine panicked and slammed on the brakes, causing the car to skid, brushing against a "hairy monster" that was standing in the road. The women screamed, the vehicle's horn sounded and the "thing" ran off into the woods.

The women later stated that the engine of the car had stalled when Christine had suddenly applied the brakes and the monster then reached inside the car and grabbed the driver's head, slamming it against the door post. Men from a nearby farmhouse ran to the scene, but the creature was nowhere to be seen. The roadway was gravel-surfaced and no footprints were visible. A short while later, Miss Van Acker's eye began to swell and turn black.

That and several other reports of sightings of a man-like monster had occurred in the same locality over a period of several weeks and then a report came in that confused the issue altogether. David Thomas, age 23, claimed that he had been grabbed by a monster three heads taller than himself and thrown to the ground. He claimed that he had escaped in his automobile. He then produced some strange-looking hairs from the vehicle's grill as evidence. When the hairs turned out to be paint brush bristles he back-tracked somewhat and admitted the whole thing could have been a hoax.

Station WFOB of Fostoria then hired a polygraph expert and had Christine, Mrs. Owens, Mrs. Bush and a neighbor, Mr. John Mays, tested on the lie detector. The result of the test was summed up in the statement that "they had seen something that had frightened them very badly."

The continuing publicity surrounding the incidents was creating quite a problem for the police, as great numbers of would-be monster hunters showed up in the area, violating private property rights, trampling growing crops and endangering local residents with their firearms. On August 23, just three days after the previous test, Christine and her mother were given a polygraph test by the Michigan State Police. The police then issued the statement that "it is our opinion that they are not telling the truth."

One other item of information that has created further skepticism regarding that incident is that David Thomas turns out to be a relative of Christine's. Could it be that they were all involved in an elaborate hoax? There had been a number of people in that area who had reported seeing giant ape-men during a period of several weeks prior to the incidents above described. Perhaps that had been enough to set the hoaxers to work, but if so, what about those original sighting reports?

It is unfortunate that no physical evidence is available to substantiate the women's account because something strange seems to be going on in Michigan. Although it is a heavily-populated state, it has great areas of forest and numerous lakes. Perhaps time will tell us more from that area.

Mass Hysteria

It has been suggested that once Bigfoot became the subject of popular magazine articles and television shows, most of the alleged sightings could then be accounted for as cases of mass hysteria. To support that belief, it is often argued that since the public has become aware of the Bigfoot/Sasquatch stories, the number of reports has grown enormously and reports have come from such unlikely areas as the Midwest and the East.

Like the hoax theory, this might very well explain some small percentage of the claimed sightings. With tales of Bigfoot fresh in his mind, a tenderfoot camper or hunter, already a bit apprehensive about being in the woods alone, might well imagine the rest.

It has been pointed out that once-alleged descriptions of the giants were published in some detail, all subsequent eye-witness reports must be held in some suspicion.

The fact is that no widespread circulation of written descriptions were published until Sanderson's books was produced in 1961. Added to that, many of the eye-witnesses were people of a type least likely to have read the book or to have ever heard of Sanderson. Many eye-witnesses report that they had never heard of the giants before the sighting took place, and are greatly relieved to find that others have reported similar sightings.

Unfortunately for the hysteria theorists, a very large percentage of sightings are claimed by solid, reliable people who are familiar with wildlife and who have spent a great part of their lives in the woods.

One example is the letter I received from Mrs. Robert Behme of Magalia, California. She stated that their sighting occurred about midnight, April 16, 1969, as she and her husband were driving between Paradise and Stirling City, California. As their car slowed, rounding a curve, their headlights shone on a "man" over six-feet-tall, covered in short black hair flecked with either white hairy patches or with mud. As the creature walked across the road in front of them, it turned to look toward them. At that time they observed that the face was white and hairless, although the features could not be clearly seen. The Behme's returned to the spot the next morning, but found no tracks in the hard-packed soil.

Mr. Behme is a writer and photographer specializing in outdoor stories and animal photography. The Behme's are both naturalists, well familiar with the wildlife of North America.

Mistaken Identity

The sighting incident just described is also an excellent argument against the frequently advanced theory that what people are really seeing are upright-walking bears. Considering his professional background, it would seem beyond reason to expect Mr. Behme to mistake a bear for a giant ape-man.

Reminding the reader of a few simple zoological facts should set the matter aside rather quickly. To begin with, the bear is a quadruped of the family Ursidae. He possesses a long snout, long thick neck and clearly visible ears. Most Bigfoot descriptions agree that it is a bipedal primate-like thing with a flat face, little or no neck and the ears are not visible.

As for footprints, the bear's hind prints might, on occasion, under just the right set of circumstances, look somewhat similar to some Bigfoot tracks. That goes for the rear footprints only, and keep in mind that the bear is a four-footed animal whose leg and pelvic structure was not designed for upright walking. Smokey Bear posters to the contrary, bears do not ordinarily amble along on their hind legs. Yes, I know, they do rise up on two legs to catch peanuts in the zoo or to peer over a berry bush at an intruder in the wild, but they do not, as a rule, walk in such a posture. So far as I can learn, in every Bigfoot sighting wherein the creature was running or walking, it was doing so in a two-legged, upright position.

In size, many Bigfoot tracks demonstrate that they are in a completely different class than any known species of bear. It has been suggested that purported Bigfoot tracks are really those of bears with deformed feet, possibly as a result of forest fires. If so, an amazing number of bears, all over the U.S. and Canada have suffered nearly identical injuries.

The possibility that an escaped gorilla has sometimes been mistaken for a Bigfoot is a matter that has been throughly investigated by researchers. To my knowledge no one has unearthed a single report of a large ape of any kind having escaped from a zoo, circus train or any other type of captivity. Needless to say, a number of escapees would be required to account for the hundreds of reports from all over North America.

The ape theory has several other drawbacks that surely eliminate it from the realm of possibility. To begin with, we once again face the problem of a four-footed beast. Like the bear, the gorilla is often pictured in an upright stance, but also like the bear, he is designed strictly for a quadrupedal gait. The gorilla's legs are quite short and comparatively weak, useful for little more than a staggering rush when bluffing an intruder. Throughout his normal activities, the gorilla and the other *pongids*, as well, travel on all fours, which means that any footprints left will also show knuckle marks nearby. In no single report of Bigfoot tracks received by us, has any hint of knuckle marks been described.

We know, also, that the giant footprints have been appearing for many years, but in conversation with an animal trainer, I learned that keeping a gorilla healthy under the best of conditions is difficult. The possibility that such a beast could survive even one cold winter in the damp forests is most unlikely according to my informant. He points out that they are particularly susceptible to respiratory infections.

It is also important to remember that all Indian stories and legends regarding the "Hairy Devils" refer to them as human or man-like things. In none of the tribal stories are they described as animals.

With surprising frequency we hear the theory advanced that the whole business is caused by a "big Indian" or a "hairy hermit" wandering around in the woods. The enormous geographical range involved is enough to make that suggestion seem foolish.

Publicity Seekers

In their energetic and sometimes frantic search for an

explanation of the ape-man phenomenon, many skeptics eventually settle for the idea that the sighting reports are all fabrications. They point out that many people have sufficient ego-need to cause them to tell the stories simply for the attention they receive. Others, it is suggested, may gain or hope to gain financially from the telling and re-telling of a fanciful story concerning a Bigfoot encounter.

A homicide detective of my acquaintance has suggested that the publicity itself is sufficient to cause certain weird personality types to claim sightings that never actually happened. He points out that in highly-publicized murder cases, it is not uncommon for innocent people to go to the police with the "confessions" simply for the feeling of importance derived from the attention they receive by so doing.

The great number of sighting reports in our files is sufficient to cast doubt upon that explanation. Are we to believe that all of those loggers, hunters, fishermen, farmers, housewives, students, boy scouts, miners and all the others are really just publicity-seeking liars? That is a pretty tall order even for a skeptical old cop like me.

That suggestion becomes almost laughable when I recall the difficulty we often have just getting some witnesses to talk. In many cases, by the time we hear the story, the witness has already suffered enough ridicule to make him quite reluctant to re-tell it.

An excellent example of that attitude was the case of Lenart Strand of Columbia, California, who claimed to have sighted a 10-foot-tall "man" on the west slope of the Sierras in 1963. That particular interview stands out in my mind for two reasons. One is that Mr. Strand was the first eye-witness I had interviewed on the Bigfoot subject. The other reason that it was a memorable experience was that it was one of the most difficult interviews I've done. Strand simply did not want to talk about it anymore. The press had been less than objective in reporting the incident and Strand's reputation and, thereby, his flying business had suffered as a result.

I held my conversation with Strand in the office of his Columbia Flying Service at the airport between Columbia and Sonora, California. I was eventually successful in convincing Strand to talk, but the conversation we did have was not taped because I felt that he would not talk freely if on tape. As well as I can remember it, the interview went as follows:

The Stockton and Sacramento papers reported on March 1, 1963, that you and your co-pilot sighted a strange thing not far from here. What can you tell me about this "thing?"

Strand: *I don't know what it was. A man of some kind covered with hair and very large.*

How did you happen to see it in the first place?

Strand: *My assistant and I were flying snow patrol for the Forest Service. We fly over certain spots in the Sierras where they have placed markers. By determining the height of the snow on them they can figure the snow depth and from that the probable runoff the following spring.*

Was there snow on the ground where you saw the creature?

Strand:*Yes, that was a year of very heavy snows and we were observing many tracks of animals that had come down to very low altitudes.*

Was this pretty far down?

Strand: Yes, just a couple of miles south of Twaine Harte, not far from Sonora. We first noticed its tracks and realized that they weren't bear tracks or anything like what we had seen before. Then we saw it standing in the snow in a clearing.

Then there was no chance it could have been a bear?

Strand: I have seen hundreds of bears while flying over this country and there is no possibility that we were mistaken. That thing was standing upright looking at us.

Can you describe it in more detail?

Strand: It was about 10- or 11-feet-tall, covered with shaggy brown or yellow-brown hair all over, kind of dirty brown. It had very broad shoulders and a tapered body.

Did it have a neck and could you see facial features?

Strand: It looked like it had no neck at all and I could see that it had a face rather than a snout, but I couldn't tell about the features.

How did you determine the height?

Strand: We had a fellow go to the same spot and stand there the next day, while we flew over again from the same altitude.

Did you get just the one look at the creature?

Strand: No, after we first spotted it I came around for a low pass so my passenger could get a picture. We were in a low-wing plane and when I tilted the wing so he could get a shot he had trouble bracing himself and operating the camera at the same time. All we got was a blur, mostly of snow.

What was the beast's reaction to the low flying

plane?

Strand: On our low pass he held up his arm as if to ward off the plane. When we came around for another look, he was gone.

Have you ever seen anything like it before or since?

Strand: No, and I have been flying over this country for many years. One thing is sure, though, if I ever see another one I am not going to tell anyone unless I get a good picture to prove it. In my business you can't afford to have people thinking you are a nut.

Mr. Strand then drew me a sketch of the creature, depicting a very broad-shouldered, tapered body, with the head set solidly on the shoulders with no evidence of a neck.

In reference to the profit motive, I can't think of anyone who has made money as the result of a Bigfoot sighting. Roger Patterson made a little money as a result of his encounter in Bluff Creek in 1967, but it was the sale of the film rights and not the sighting itself that was profitable. It sometimes happens that reporting a monster sighting can result in economic loss. The case of Verlin Herrington is an example.

Herrington was a deputy sheriff of Gray's Harbor County, Washington when he claimed to have seen a Bigfoot on July 26, 1969. He stated that he was driving home at 2:30 a.m. when he saw the creature standing alongside the road near Hoquiam. He described it as very large, covered with dark hair and with prominent breasts. The face was flat and leathery. He told me that the creature did not move as he stopped and covered it with a spotlight. When he stepped out of his car and cocked his revolver the beast turned and walked into the forest.

When I talked to Herrington on the telephone, he admitted that his sheriff was very angry with him for having made the report. It had received nationwide publicity and the sheriff felt his department had been embarrassed by the whole incident. Later, in speaking to several other deputies of the same department, I was told that Herrington, who was a temporary summer employee, probably would not be re-hired the following summer.

Certainly a percentage of sighting reports may be prevarications, for whatever reason. I believe, however, that the percentage is extremely low. I like to believe that I learned something in a quarter century of law enforcement, and one of those things is the ability to interrogate intelligently. Policemen are lied to nearly every day and so, of necessity, must learn techniques of witness interrogation that aid in determining the facts.

As most any good cop might do, immediately after hearing a Bigfoot story, I make it a point to learn what I can about the witness or witnesses. I may have offended some of the witnesses in so doing, but I have always felt it important to learn something of the witness' reputation for honesty, sobriety and stability. The majority of the people in question are residents of rural areas where a reputation as a liar, drunkard or screwball is not likely to be kept secret.

In the great majority of cases, I have found the alleged witness to be of good reputation. In those few cases where I found otherwise, the story had sounded a little fishy, anyway.

A recent television documentary devoted to the subject of Bigfoot, the Yeti and the Loch-Ness Monster included a segment wherein a psychiatrist made some comments relative to the monster phenomenon. He stated, and with a straight face, too, that the reason people think they are seeing Bigfoot and other monsters is because people want to believe in them. He feels that these subjects have become more prominent in the news of late because the public is seeking escape from the boredom of modern life and belief in monsters is exciting to them.

It may be that some bored residents of megalopolis may think the idea of ape-men in North America is great fun, On the other hand, those who live in rural, mountainous regions, as I do, may well feel differently. My neighbor, Gene Putnam, an employee of the Department of Natural Resources, spends his entire work day in the forest, often alone. I'm certain that he would rather not think about 8-foot-tall, 900-pound man-things inhabiting those forests!

Mental Gymnastics

In order to explain away the more than one thousand reports of footprints and sightings, the confirmed skeptic must, when faced with the evidence, turn to some far fetched, mind-stretching "solutions."

The matter of the hoax has been pretty thoroughly discussed and although obviously an explanation in a very few cases, it simply breaks down when applied to the majority of cases. Its two most serious drawbacks being that (a) in only two instances in our files has a prank been admitted or proven and (b) some footprints have obviously been faked and a few alleged sightings may have been fabrications, but often tracks and sightings are reported in the same case and by different witnesses.

The explanations relating to mis-identification might be valid in a tiny percentage of instances wherein the witness was unfamiliar with the appearance of bears in the wild. It should also be kept in mind that the tracks so often reported in conjunction with sightings are definitely not bear tracks. The explanation that purported Bigfoot tracks are really just the prints of bears, foxes or other animals that have melted out is also possibly true in a very few cases. That argument is weak because of the fact that the majority of tracks have been found in mud, dust or sand rather than in snow. In fact, judging by the proportionately small number of footprints found in the wintertime, it appears that Bigfoot is much less active and possibly hibernates to some extent.

The other often repeated "explanations" are seen to break down upon logical consideration of the facts. Again, in some few instances, some of them may be valid. What we finally must admit is that a very small percentage of Bigfoot reports are not Bigfoot reports at all. Quite the opposite situation, as a matter of fact, than that faced by the UFO researcher who finds that the majority of his reports can be crossed off as normal happenings.

Obviously, if only a few alleged Sasquatch/Bigfoot reports can be dismissed as fakes or mistakes, then the majority of those that remain must be genuine reports describing strange beasts. Or, to put it another way, if only one set of foot prints or only one sighting is genuine, the fact that all the others are fake is of no consequence.

Chapter 5
In Our Own Backyard

I have devoted a full chapter to the so-called "Bossburg Incidents" for several, hopefully sound, reasons. To begin with, it's a good story, typical of Sasquatchery in some ways, amazingly different in others. It is also important because the "cripple-foot" tracks that were part of the 1969 Bossburg happenings appear to have convinced some people that Bigfoot is a subject for serious study. Last, but certainly not least, is my somewhat selfish interest in those events because we now live little more than a stone's throw from where many of the tracks and sightings were reported.

Perhaps Stevens County, Washington would be a more appropriate title, because all of the sightings and some of the tracks were actually reported from areas outside the immediate Bossburg area. Bossburg was, however, the headquarters for most of the Bigfoot researchers who were drawn to the scene. Bossburg, by the way, is a tiny village along the Columbia River about

20 miles north of Colville, county seat of Stevens County in Northeastern Washington. Although quite beautiful in the spring and fall, this corner of the state is bitterly cold in winter and hot and dry in the summer. It is a land of gentle hills and low mountains—forested, for the most part.

There are alfalfa and cattle ranches in the valleys. Unlike many areas to the west in the Cascades and north in British Columbia, there is little wilderness here, There are few places that cannot be reached during the dry months, at least by four-wheel-drive vehicles.

As in so many other areas of concentrated Bigfoot activity, there seem to have been several distinct periods to the investigation beginning when the first reports received nationwide newspaper coverage and caused an influx of Bigfoot hunters. Then there was a period in which additional activity was reported during which research disclosed that occasional Bigfoot incidents had been reported over a period of many years. Finally, the present state of affairs in which little or no activity is being reported and the Sasquatch seekers have moved on to greener pastures.

A Quiet Beginning

It has been suggested that the unusually severe winter of 1969-70 was in some way responsible for the fact that Bigfoot showed up so regularly in Northeastern Washington. That is perhaps possible, but our records indicate that the Sasquatch "invasion" actually started during the spring months of 1969, although they attracted little attention at the time.

In early spring, exact date unknown, Mrs. Betty Peterson of Kettle Falls reported that two giant ape-men ran across the road as she was driving near Orient.

Orient is across the Columbia River and just a few miles northwest of Bossburg. Mrs. Peterson stated that the creatures were black, both over 7-feet-tall and they leaned forward slightly when they ran. Her report is particularly interesting because the sighting occurred at 11:00 a.m. and she was able to see both creatures quite clearly.

In April, a woman driving toward Colville sighted two of the giants apparently eating from trash cans at Williams Lake Road and the Columbia River Road, about 5 miles north of Bossburg. The witness drove to Colville and notified the sheriff's department, but apparently no record was made of the incident and the identity of the witness is unknown at this time.

Along about the same time, tracks began showing up in the hills near Bossburg and there was an unconfirmed report of a sighting near the garbage cans at the Williams Lake Campground.

It was not until November 1969, however, that the incidents began to attract any but local attention. On November 24, Joe Rhodes, a Colville butcher found Bigfoot tracks in the soft soil near the Bossburg garbage dump. Particularly interesting is the fact that the prints indicated that the creature had one badly-deformed foot. The left footprint measured almost 18 inches in length and was a typical five-toed Sasquatch track.

The right foot was much shorter and extremely misshapen, with either two of the toes or two bones protruding off to the side.

Some researchers feel that it is important to note that it was about the same time that Ivan Marx, part-time big game guide, part-time Bigfoot hunter, took up residence in Bossburg. It has been suggested by some that Ivan may have been responsible for some of the tracks, although to my knowledge, there has never been any proof offered to substantiate the charge. Those who have accused Marx of faking the Bossburg prints are perhaps unaware that tracks of the cripple-foot creature have been reported in Northeastern Washington for many years.

Marx apparently felt that the creature was handicapped to the extent that it was forced to live off of garbage and, therefore, should be easy enough to capture or kill.

He notified Rene Dahinden who was, at the time, busy checking on a sighting report near Nordegg, Saskatchewan.

Within a few days Rene arrived, followed shortly by Bob Titmus, a taxidermist and former member of the Slick expedition. A number of local enthusiasts were by then becoming active in searching for additional evidence. Among them were Norm Davis of Colville radio station KCVL, Don Byington, who had discovered some tracks on his ranch near Bossburg, and my good friend Bob Hewes, whose 18-foot power boat would be used extensively by Bigfoot hunters in the following weeks.

On December 14, Dahinden and Titmus found tracks of the cripple-foot creature leading out of and back into the Columbia River about 6 miles north of Bossburg.

The creature had apparently climbed out of the river up a steep bank in the snow. It had then crossed the highway and a railroad track and wandered around on a hillside before returning to the river.

Dahinden counted a total of 1,087 footprints in that trail. In one instance, the creature obviously stepped over a 43-inch barbed-wire fence.

Dahinden, Marx and Titmus have been criticized for wasting so much time counting and studying the tracks, when they obviously had a Sasquatch walking or limping around Stevens County, waiting to be caught. Dahinden has defended his actions with the statement that they wanted to assure themselves that the tracks were genuine before investing any great amounts of time and effort.

Five days later, a U.S. border patrolman discovered what appeared to be tracks of the same creature. They were partially destroyed by rain. Those tracks were found across the river and about 2 miles upriver.

No matter what the reason, Dahinden's failure to get hot on the trail upset Norm Davis who felt the hunt was being neglected. He notified every Bigfoot hunter he could contact. Shortly thereafter, most of the active Bigfoot investigators in the country arrived. They included Roger Patterson and his partner, Dennis Jensen, Roger St. Hilaire, and eventually John Green and Peter Byrne.

That was the first time that so many Bigfoot investigators had combined forces in a single area . Perhaps "combined forces" is not an appropriate description of the working arrangement because, as time went on, there appeared to be a decided lack of cooperation and trust among the Bigfooters. Perhaps that is not surprising. Each of them had, on his own, spent tremendous amounts of time and energy and all available funds in years of fruitless search. Now, with a hot, fresh trail, each wanted to be the man to bring in a Sasquatch. An event occurred near the end of January that made matters worse—much worse.

Act One: The Frisco Fiasco

After weeks of searching the area without further

success, the hunters were about to give up and move on. Then, a local prospector named Joe Metlow arrived at the hunters' camp and asked how much they would give him for a Sasquatch! He explained that he had very recently seen one digging roots, at a location he refused to divulge, and that he believed the creature was living at that particular location.

Metlow actually made his announcement to the Dahinden and Marx group, but it was not long before the Patterson and Jensen bunch heard about it. Although Metlow was remaining very evasive about the location of the creature, he received cash offers from both camps to lead them to the specimen. Two things about those cash offers are worthy of comment. To begin with, it seems strange that experienced Sasquatchers, knowing the extreme mobility of the creatures, would bother with monetary offers at all. The chance that "Metlow's Monster" would hang around and wait for the deal to be consummated was remote, indeed. That apparently did not occur to either camp and neither did the fact that none of them had the kind of money they were offering! It was rumored that the bids eventually reached $50,000 or more.

Patterson then notified Tom Page, a wealthy Ohio Businessman who he knew would be willing to pay for a Sasquatch, dead or alive. Page flew to Colville, immediately.

Things began to take on the atmosphere of a low-budget spy movie. Metlow was followed everywhere he went and his followers were being trailed by still others. Added to the scene was the fact that Norm Davis, the radio station owner, and Denny Striker of the *Colville Statesman-Examiner* were following everybody. They, at least were acting in a professional manner. There appeared to be a gigantic scoop in the making and they were, after all, newsmen.

Meanwhile, Metlow, who had started it all, had still not disclosed the location of his monster. When Page offered him $1,000 to name the location, he stated that it was on Frisco Mountain. It is doubtful that any money actually changed hands, but Metlow apparently knew the time had come to quit stalling. He named a location— somewhere on Frisco Mountain, about thirty miles north of Colville. Immediately Page and his group flew to the mountain in a helicopter and spent the day on snowshoes without finding a trace of the creature. They later reported that they had been followed by a private plane that had buzzed them repeatedly during the day. It was, presumably, the Dahinden faction.

This ridiculous situation grew even more so when Metlow began changing his story. He then claimed he actually had a Sasquatch carcass and in fact had parts of it in his freezer.

When his bluff was called on that claim, he admitted that he did not have anything in his freezer, but he did have a Sasquatch foot in his sister's freezer in Portland. When pressed to make good on that claim, Metlow just faded out of the picture and the Sasquatch hunters finally got back to business.

By that time, John Green had arrived on the scene and attempted to get the entire investigation back on a more professional course. I had been unable to leave my duties with the Los Angeles Sheriff's Department and considering some of the things that happened in the Bossburg business, I am almost relieved to find that I missed it all.

There were three more sets of tracks found in Stevens County during the spring and summer. One was a set of tracks in the snow near Arden, about 5 miles south of Colville.

One researcher followed them for several miles into the Pend Orielle game range before losing them in the patchy spring snow. A second, and much more highly-publicized set of prints, was found near the highway at Arden just a few days later. The second set proved to be the work of hoaxer, Ray Pickens, who claimed to have made "all the tracks." Interrogation of Pickens by several Bigfoot investigators made it evident that Pickens was not even aware of many of the tracks that had been found in past months.

Unfortunately, Picken's story led many of the local people to believe the whole Sasquatch thing had been a joke. Unfortunately, that attitude still prevails in the area and is making our present investigative efforts most difficult.

On July 3, 1970, Norm Davis's daughter found 18-inch tracks in the mud at North Gorge Campground near Bossburg. For many weeks after, that no other evidence was reported from the Bossburg area and most of the investigators left. Marks and Jensen had both moved to Bossburg with their families. Both families remained, not so much because of Sasquatch as the fact that they liked the area. Jensen went to work in a local lumber mill and, as we shall see, Marx also kept busy.

Act Two: The Marx Movie

In October, Marx notified Rene Dahinden that he had a Sasquatch on film. The Bossburg-Colville area was soon over-run with Sasquatch hunters once again. The wire services got on the story and it looked like the whole scene was about to repeat itself.

What Marx had come up with was a couple of minutes of 16mm film showing a large, black, upright, furry creature moving through the forest. It was obviously injured, with both ankles bleeding and its right arm held tightly against the chest.

The object in the film eventually reached a clearing with the cameraman following. Even though it turned to look toward the cameraman on two occasions the facial features were not clear.

Marx claimed to have made the film while tracking the creature with his hunting dogs on October 7th. The previous night, according to Marx, he had received an anonymous call informing him that a Bigfoot had been struck, either by a car or a train and was in the area injured.

Most of the Bigfoot hunters who viewed the film felt that it was not only authentic, but by far the most impressive evidence ever obtained. The many local people who had an opportunity to see it were also impressed and interest in and enthusiasm for the whole Sasquatch situation was re-kindled, temporarily.

As mentioned earlier, one of the locals who had assisted the investigators was Bossburg rancher, Don Byington. After one of the showings of the film Don's sons commented that they recognized the background in the most important scene, the one where the creature crosses a clearing. Marx had not been particularly specific about the location where the pictures had been taken, but had commented that the nearby tree branches indicated the creature was about 9-feet-tall.

After learning of the actual location of the filming, several investigators checked the immediate area and took a few measurements. The result was a unanimous agreement that the creature had been closer to 6 feet than 9 feet in height. Certain other details of the sight seemed to conflict with statements made by Marx, so considerable doubt was cast upon the authenticity of the film.

Marx later claimed to have taken and passed a lie detector test relative to the filming, but there seems to be no confirmation of that statement. Several significant points come to mind when considering the possibility of a hoax. First, if genuine, that film would be, because of its clarity, far more valuable to the scientific world than the Patterson film. Yet, there is no record so far as I can learn of any showing before a scientific group.

The film, if genuine, would presumably be of considerable monetary value, yet Marx has apparently never made any money from the sale of the film or any part of it.

It is also interesting to note that Marx has had very little to say in defense of the film and has since made at least one other of similar questionable quality.

So, once again, the Bigfoot investigators, hunters and "movie-makers" moved on to other parts. Bossburg and the rest of Stevens County returned to normal, with the citizenry firmly convinced that Bigfoot and Bigfoot hunters were a joke and not a particularly funny one at at that.

The Cripple-Foot Tracks

Those particular tracks and certain other aspects of the Bossburg events are worthy of closer scrutiny, if for no other reason than the fact that those events did what other Bigfoot incidents had failed to do. They attracted the attention of the scientific world.

Dr. John Napier, one of the world's leading anthropologists, published a book in 1971 titled *Bigfoot, the Yeti and the Sasquatch In Myth and Reality.* Apparently Dr. Napier had previously demonstrated an open-mind on the subject as he was one of the few who took the time to view the Patterson film. Dr. Napier's book deals with both the Yeti of Asia and the Sasquatch of North America, and it is obvious from his comments that he feels that the latter does, indeed, exist.

Interestingly, it was the Bossburg cripple-foot tracks that he found most convincing of all Bigfoot evidence so far collected. He comments on the fact that the club foot appears very authentic for a disability of that kind. He points out out how unlikely it seems that a hoaxer would be knowledgeable enough and sick enough to fake a footprint of that nature.

So, in the long run, those tracks of the Bossburg club-foot may prove to be the most important of all the thousands of possible ape-man tracks so far seen photographed and cast.

I have heard stories among the old-time residents hereabouts that tell of those tracks having been seen from time to time for many years. I have so far been unable to trace any of those stories to an actual eye witness.

Those tracks are interesting in other ways. They were first reported near the Bossburg garbage dump on October 24, 1969. The tracks led from the dump toward the Columbia River. Three weeks later Dahinden and Titmus found the 1,087 tracks that emerged from the Columbia a few miles north of Bossburg. In that instance, the creature climbed up a steep bank, then wandered around the hillside for nearly a mile before returning to the river.

That was in mid-December, of one of the coldest winters in the history of Northeastern Washington. The Columbia, at that point, is actually called Lake Roosevelt as it is backed up behind Grand Coulee Dam. The lake is a couple of miles wide there and must have been near freezing at the time. If Bigfoot was actually slopping about in the river, as the evidence indicates, then he must be a mighty tough hombre.

Considering the tracks that were found across the river and those found later at the nearby North Gorge Campground, it would appear that "Cripple-Foot" uses the Columbia as a thoroughfare. The thought then comes to mind that he might habitually travel by water because his deformity makes overland travel difficult. Many Sasquatch reports describe the creatures either wading or swimming and a very large percentage of tracks are found near lakes and rivers.

On the night in question, (December 13), he apparently left the river by climbing up a fairly steep, snow covered bank. He crossed a railroad track and the highway then walked around over the nearby hillsides, before returning to the river. He re-entered the river at a point near where he had climbed out. Marks in the snow indicated that he had slid down the bank on his bottom much as a youngster would do in playing in the snow.

Because that is one of the longest series of Bigfoot prints yet found it is interesting to note the creature's apparent activities during that stroll. As has been indicated, at one point he stepped over a forty three inch high fence, apparently without leaving any fur in the barbs. At another point there is a large depression in the snow where a large animal had apparently lain.

One item of evidence that definitely should have been collected was a large, yellowed section of snow where the creature had apparently urinated. I have never heard any explanation as to why that potentially valuable evidence was not collected.

Bob Hewes had the opportunity to examine the area of the tracks quite thoroughly and observed a most interesting set of circumstances. He pointed out that the creature walked up to and in some cases, around fir trees and apparently ate the tender fir tip buds from the trees. Bob commented on that apparent fact to the Bigfoot hunters at the scene, but they all felt there was no connection between the tracks and the tiny husks from the fir buds that were lying nearby in considerable quantities. Bob, nevertheless, is quite convinced that Cripple-Foot was munching on the delicacy. Hardly a meal for a giant, but perhaps a highly favored tidbit.

Bob also commented on the fake tracks at Arden. He admits those tracks were very difficult to distinguish from the real thing, especially because they were several days old when he first saw them. He points out that they had one very tell-tale characteristic, however. That is, they started at the edge of the road and returned to nearly the same spot. On the other hand, every convincing set of prints he has seen, emerged from the woods or water and disappeared in some similar spot.

The Continuing Story

The Bossburg events of 1969-70 attracted perhaps more attention from the press, Bigfoot hunters, and even some scientists than any similar situation has ever done. Yet, in studying the local situation I find that those incidents were only part of a continuing story of ape-man activity in this part of Northwest Washington.

I recently heard the story of a sighting by several local men that is supposed to have occurred 20 years ago. It was early morning and the men were deer hunting. One of the hunters was unable to do much hiking due to a heart condition. His companions stationed him on a mountain ridge, near the road and then went down into a nearby canyon to drive the deer toward him.

A short while later, the men returned to their companion and who excitedly described to them an "ape" they had flushed from the forest. The hunter who had been stationed on the hill then explained that the creature had run right past him and that he had been too startled to do anything but sit and watch as it disappeared in the forest.

Most interesting is the location of that incident, Frisco Mountain! I wonder if Metlow had heard that story, too? Then again, maybe Metlow really did have something after all. Another sighting report from the 1950s has, as a location, the Leadpoint area, almost within the shadow of Frisco Mountain. The exact date and circumstances are unknown, but there are a number of local residents who clearly remember hearing of the incident.

A man and his son reported finding 18-inch tracks near Republic, which is across the river and due west of Bossburg.

Tracks were found in the snow west of Orient, December 21, 1968. Just six months later, the Peterson sighting occurred near Orient as described earlier.

By the end of 1970, the Bigfoot investigators had

come and gone once again and even Ivan Marx had moved on to new adventures. For that reason it is almost humorous to note the location of the next report in our Northeast Washington file. Tracks were found in the hills above Bossburg, not far from where Marx had lived.

According to Peter Byrne, in the early part of 1972, a sighting was reported across the river, near Sherman Pass. No other details are available regarding that particular incident.

In late November 1972, a member of our investigative group found old, indistinct tracks in the Rocky Creek area, a few miles north of Colville.

Tracks were reportedly found in November 1973, southwest of Colville near the river. I did not hear of that report until several months later and so was unable to investigate. The tracks were described as very large with one badly deformed foot.

Another report received too late to allow any active field work was made by a woman who had seen tracks while out hunting for a Christmas tree in December 1973. She described the tracks to me and sketched them. They were typical "hourglass"-shaped Bigfoot prints, 17-inches long, but with only three toes showing. She stated that it appeared that the foot was designed for five toes, but that only three seemed to print. In other words, the foot "had room" for the remaining toes. The informant claimed to know little or nothing about Bigfoot and was evidently quite surprised when I showed her photographs of footprints with that same hourglass shape. The location of the tracks was about 15 miles east of Colville. It had snowed several times in the month since she had seen the tracks, but she pointed out to us where the tracks had left the creek and crossed the road before continuing up the hill into the forest.

As I write this I can look out over the forested mountains toward Bossburg and I can't help thinking about those "cripple-foot" tracks. Somewhere out there in those snow-covered woods there is very possibly a hairy man-monster limping along on a club foot. He must be quite a fellow, judging by the size of his footprints.

The good foot is almost 18-inches long. This ape-man must be one of the largest of all such creatures. He is certainly hardy, judging by his ability to sleep in the open in midwinter and his willingness to swim in extremely cold water. He must be old and tough.

Chapter 6
The Evidence
A detailed analysis of the sightings, footprints and other evidence.

The many ape-men incidents described in preceding chapters have, of necessity, been dealt with in a somewhat cursory manner. At this point I will describe and discuss some of those incidents in greater detail. By so doing, the reader will be given the opportunity to gain a clearer understanding of the remarkable phenomenon with which we are dealing.

As the years have gone by and our file of information has grown, it has become increasingly clear to some of us that we are, in fact, dealing with not one, but several types of ape-men on the North American continent. Most of the presently active investigators started out in search of Sasquatch and Bigfoot of the Northwest. Particularly in the past three or four years, we have become ever more aware of the fact that there are "other things" out there.

The bulk of the information collected concerns those creatures popularly called Bigfoot or Sasquatch. For that reason, this detailed analysis of evidence will concern itself with those creatures. The following chapter will attempt to bring some order out of the confusion of information relating to those other creatures. For purposes of clarity and simplicity, they will be referred to hereafter by terms describing their specific characteristics.

Surprisingly, the most common evidence is the nearly 600 eye-witness accounts of encounters with Bigfoot. That figure is surprising because one normally expects the tracks, feces and other signs of a wild creature to be more often observed than the creatures themselves. The cougar, or mountain lion, is an excellent example. I have talked to many people who have spent their lives in the backwoods country who have never seen a cougar, but have on many occasions observed their tracks.

The fact that we have more reports of sightings than tracks may or may not indicate that the giants make an effort to avoid leaving tracks at times. There are a few incidents where that would appear to be the case, but the opposite is true in the majority of instances. It is quite possible that many Bigfoot tracks go unnoticed in the dry months of the year because the terrain in which they live does not lend itself to good tracking.

Although Bigfoot tracks have, at times, been observed in the mulch of the forest floor, they are not easily seen even by someone specifically looking for tracks of that kind.

There have been over 500 sets of footprints reported. They, certainly, are of sufficient number to allow an in-depth study of those prints and the variations to be found.

Several sets of possible Sasquatch hair samples have been collected and at least two samples of possible Sasquatch feces. Laboratory analysis of those samples have been conducted.

Because the sighting reports are the most common type of evidence, we can start our examination of the file with some examples of sightings that contain detailed descriptions of the creatures. In October 1955, Mr. William Roe was hiking in the mountains near Tete Juane Cache, B.C. when he sighted his monster. Although he was not hunting, he was armed with a rifle since he had killed a grizzly bear in the same area the previous year. About three in the afternoon, he came to a little clearing and observed on the other side of the clearing what appeared to be the head and shoulders of a grizzly among some low bushes. Roe decided to conceal himself in the brush and so he sat on a rock to observe the beast. As it turned, the creature entered the clearing, walking toward him, he observed that it was no bear at all, but was generally humanoid in form. It was apparently a female with long hanging breasts and it walked upright. The creature had not yet seen him as it began eating leaves, stripping them from the branches with its teeth. It then apparently caught sight of him and turned and walked rapidly away, disappearing into the forest after emitting a whinnying-type of cry.

Mr. Roe, in his sworn statement also commented that the monster did not seem terribly frightened of him and that he could have easily shot it, but did not do so because it was so human in appearance. He stated that he attempted to follow it into the forest and did succeed in catching one more glimpse of it. He also reported finding droppings in several places and found one place where it had apparently slept in the open. He examined the feces and so far as he was able to determine, it contained only vegetable matter.

Mr. Roe's description of the creature is particularly valuable for its detail. He compared it with the Patterson pictures, which was a female too. In his report, Roe describes the monster as about 6 feet tall and near 300 pounds, but in a later statement, he estimates the weight at about 500 pounds. He further stated that she had a broad thick body and was covered from head to foot with dark brown, silver-tipped hair. The arms were heavier than a man's and longer—reaching almost to its knees. The eyes were small and black and the teeth, white and even. The head was higher in the back than in the front. The nose was flat, and the only places bare of hair were around the nose, mouth and ears. The ears were human-shaped and the neck much shorter and thicker than a human's.

Also important when comparing this sighting with the Patterson movie is Roe's statement that the creature placed the heel of its foot down first when walking. He also stated that the soles of the feet were grey-brown and the feet broader than a man's, tapering to thinner heels.

On August 26, 1957, Mr. Roe made an official sworn affidavit, declaring the truth of the statement. That was done, I believe, at the request of John Green.

I think it is important to note that the sworn statement was made two years after he originally told the story. There is no evidence whatever that Roe obtained any financial gain as a result of the publicity he received upon telling the story. There is no doubt that he did suffer more than a little ridicule, yet two years later, he was willing to file the sworn statement with the Canadian authorities. It seems that if it had been no more than a hoax to begin with, he would have been quite willing to let it drop, having achieved nothing by the telling of it.

The fact that Mr. Roe first described the incident in 1955 is important because, as far as I can learn, there had not been a detailed description of the Sasquatch published anywhere. Roe describes many details of the creature's appearance that were not again reported for many years. Many of the details of the description he gave have been substantiated in more recent sightings. There is nothing in William Roe's background to cast any doubt whatever on his story and as the years go by, and more and more evidence is obtained, his statement tends to ring ever more true. If true, his statement is, of course, sufficient to establish the presence of giant sub-hominoid creatures on the North American continent.

Perhaps the most famous, and certainly the most sensational, Sasquatch report was told by Canadian Albert Ostman. Ostman did not make his story public until after publication of Roe's encounter, although it had occurred 34 years earlier. Ostman also signed a sworn statement.

Ostman says he was alone in the rugged country east of Toba Inlet on the British Columbia coast, taking a vacation and searching for a lost gold mine. He tells how he found his camp belongings disturbed two days in a row as if something had been going through his things while he slept. He had left his knapsack hanging in a tree each night and, on the second morning, found that it had been dumped upside down and some prunes and pancake powder stolen.

The following night, he slept with his rifle and his boots inside his sleeping bag, intending to stay awake to catch his night-time visitor. However, he fell asleep and was awakened suddenly when he and his sleeping bag were suddenly lifted from the ground. He says it felt as though he had been slung over the back of a horse and carried off. He was down inside of the sleeping bag and the bag was being held partially closed. As a few minutes went by, he realized he was being carried, slung over the shoulder of someone or something, and he was in great pain due to the cramped position with the boots and rifle for company. He says he knew his abductor had also taken his packsack, as he could hear the cans rattling.

For a period of time that Ostman estimates as three hours, he was carried up mountains and down. He could hear his kidnapper breathing heavily and occasionally coughing. He was eventually dumped on the ground and managed to crawl out of the bag for some air, although his legs were too numb to walk. As he crawled out, he heard some jabbering among several individuals and looked up to see four huge creatures standing around him. Even though it was too dark to make out any details, he knew they must be the Apemen that he had heard about from the Indians. He states that the chattering sounded like some language he had never before heard.

As the light got better, he looked at his watch and found it was 4:25 a.m. He was then able to get a good look at his captors and observed that they were shaped like humans, covered with hair and with no clothes at all. They appeared to be a family; a huge male, a large female and two younger ones—a male and a female.

He further observed that he was in a bowl-shaped valley of eight or ten acres, surrounded by high mountains. At one end was an opening, where he had apparently been brought in. He took stock of his equipment and found that he had his compass and prospecting glass on strings around his neck. He also had his rifle and six cartridges.

At this point in his story Ostman, goes into considerable detail concerning which items of food had arrived there with him and which ones had disappeared. His story then continues with a lengthy description of his stay with the giants. The young ones, particularly the male, were quite curious about him. The young female seemed quite shy.

He set up camp in the valley and ate a little cold food, waiting for a chance to escape through the opening in the canyon wall. His rifle was a 30.30 and he apparently did not feel it was sufficiently powerful to kill the huge creatures. He also explained that he did not want to kill any of them as they had not harmed him.

He made several observations as to the habits of the giants that are very interesting. He states that the older female often went out for most of the day, returning with her arms full of grass and twigs from spruce and hemlock as well as some ground nuts. The young male apparently often went out and gathered some kind of grass with long, sweet roots.

Ostman stated that it was his opinion that this was only a temporary stopping place for the creatures and that they probably moved from place to place for food gathering purposes. He did note, however, that they slept in a shallow cave in the side of the mountain and the floor of the cave was covered with dry moss. He states that they slept on blankets woven of strips of cedar bark.

Because the creatures were so curious about Ostman's belongings, he was able to get them interested in his snuff.

He eventually got the old male to swallow a mouthful

of snuff which made him sick enough that Oatman was able to make a run for the opening in the mountain. He says he had to fire one shot over the head of the old female who had started to pursue him. He eventually made his way back to the coast and to a logging operation where he was fed and provided with transportation, although he did not tell the story of his capture.

If Ostman's story is factual, it is the most important of all the reports in our file because of the details of the creature's descriptions and their habits. He describes the adult male as nearly 8 feet tall with a barrel chest and a large hump on his back. His shoulders were very powerful and his biceps enormous. His forearms were very long and his hands shaped like a scoop, with comparatively short fingers and nails like chisels. Their hands, the bottoms of their feet and the area around the nose and eyes were the only places without hair. He did not see their ears as they were covered with hair.

He also noted that the soles of their feet seemed to be padded like a dog's foot with the big toe much larger than the rest and it was used in climbing.

The adult female was described as over 7 feet tall and 500 or 600 pounds. The hair on the head was about 6 inches long and the rest much shorter, but it was quite thick in some places.

He described the young male as about 7 feet tall and 300 pounds. Ostman said he had no fear of the young female, as she appeared quite harmless.

Certain other points of Ostman's story seem to agree in most ways with the descriptions given by other witnesses and by what can be observed in the Patterson film. He described their sloping foreheads and noted that the back of the head was about 4 or 5 inches higher than the front. Their jaws were wide, but the forehead quite narrow. The old male had prominent canine teeth, although Ostman points out they were not really large enough to be called fangs.

In most details, the description of the adult female is very similar to the Roe report, but the matter of visible ears is an interesting exception. Except for Roe's account, visible ears are practically unheard of in Bigfoot/Sasquatch reports.

One item of information in the Ostman account which has never, to my knowledge, been mentioned in other reports is the description of the genitals. He noted the penis of the giant to be very small and more or less covered by a fold of skin.

The following sighting report was related to me by John Green, and it apparently occurred in the late fall of 1967. The witness in this case does not want his name used, but he did put the story on tape.

The incident took place in Oregon and the weather was cold, windy and foggy. The witness was walking down a trail from the road-building job where he had been working when he began noticing something strange. He observed some good-sized rocks that were quite dry while everything else thereabouts was wet from the damp, foggy conditions.

Then he looked up on a ridge and saw several strange-looking creatures picking up rocks, turning them over and smelling of them. There were 3 of the creatures—a large male, a slightly smaller female and a young one. They appeared almost human except that they were covered with hair; the male was a dirty brown and the female, fawn-colored. The male was especially heavy through the shoulders and had much longer hair on his head than the others. They all seemed to have stooped shoulders with their heads set farther down on the chest than humans. They seemed to have little or no neck.

As the witness stood and watched, the creatures moved along a ledge covered with piles of large, flat, sharp-edged boulders. They were kneeling down most of the time, picking up the rocks, turning them over and sniffing them, then stacking them loosely in piles. Eventually, the old male seemed to find what he was looking for and pulled out a large rodent nest of some sort. They tore the nest apart and removed and ate several of the rodents that had apparently been hibernating in the nest. He states they ate the rodents in much the same way we would eat a banana.

Up until that time the giants had not been aware of his presence, but after eating, they noticed him and moved quickly but quietly into the forest and he did not see them again. The following day, the witness returned to the spot and found footprints 15 inches long and 5 inches wide, but saw no further sign of the giants.

Some months after the incident, he directed John Green to the location and pointed out the piles of rock he had described. John observed the rocks to be stacked in such a way that they could not have been a natural formation. In the spot where the witness stated they found the nest, the rocks were observed to have been lifted out leaving a hole fully 5 feet deep.

The three sighting reports just described fairly well sum up what is known about the physical appearance of the Northwest giants. We could go on from here with the nearly 600 additional sightings in our files, but much of the material would be repetitious. The reader may wish to refer to John Green's Sasquatch File for many of those additional reports.

Footprint Evidence

Many skeptics unfamiliar with the result of our research have criticized us for our belief in the existence of the giants, based on little more than "a few holes in the ground and the wild tales of drunken loggers." Even if that were all we had for evidence, it would still be sufficient to justify belief in the existence of Bigfoot.

It should be pointed out that footprint evidence can, under some circumstances, be quite reliable. That should be obvious from the fact that many criminals have gone to jail or to the gallows, based upon evidence of that type.

Keeping in mind that we are limiting our discussion to the Bigfoot/Sasquatch of the Northwest, we will discuss those "odd-looking holes in the ground."

As Dr. Napier has pointed out, Bigfoot prints seem to fall into two definite type-categories. The most common is quite properly described as hourglass-shaped. The other is called the "board foot" and has little or no arch or curve on either side, from toes to heel. Dr. Napier points out that such a degree of variation would be unlikely between individuals of the same species. He then comments that the possibility of two, heretofore unknown species of primate, inhabiting the Northwest is biologically unlikely, therefore one of the two types must be man-made.

At the time he made that statement, Dr. Napier was apparently unaware of the three-toed, four-toed, V-shaped and various other odd foot types regularly showing up in different parts of North America.

Also important is the fact that, on occasion, both the hourglass and the board foot prints have been found together. In 1960, two sets of tracks were found in the Bluff Creek. One was 15 inches long and hourglass-shaped, the other was 13 inches and board-shaped. It certainly seems unlikely that a hoaxer who came across a set of genuine prints would hurry home to construct a set of his own, then return to walk alongside the genuine tracks. We are simply going to have to assume that there is great individual variation between the foot shapes among the giants.

Because the hourglass prints are most common, we will discuss them in some detail. As will be seen by the illustrations, the prints at first look much as if they were made by very large human feet. However, upon closer examination we observe certain important details that add up to something quite unlike the human foot.

If we draw a line through the base of the Bigfoot toes, we will see that it forms either a straight line or a gentle curve. A line drawn through the base of human toes will exhibit a march sharper curve and we will note that the base of the big toe is set farther back than the others.

On the inside, or big-toe side, of the Sasquatch foot, we often find a slight bulge, or actually, a double bulge, apparently caused by a padding or webbing under the toes. That is substantiated by the fact that a close scrutiny of the footprints indicates that the axis or ball of the foot is well behind the apparent base of the toes. So what appears to be a long, fairly narrow foot with short toes is actually a short broad foot with long toes.

One anthropologist has pointed out that the ankle appears to be farther forward than in the human foot. In other words the heel is both larger and broader than in the human, resulting in the hourglass shape of the print. Such a foot structure is also a logical adaptation for a creature of great weight.

It is obvious from a study of the prints that Bigfoot does not walk just like man. In man, the weight of the body rests first on the heel, then shifts slightly toward the outside of the foot. The foot then rotates forward, eventually bringing the weight to the outside toes, where it rotates inward to push off.

It appears that the Sasquatch foot operates in a somewhat more simplified manner. The weight is first placed on the heel as in man, but then moves straight forward to the push-off.

Those specific details of Sasquatch tracks have been observed hundreds of times throughout northwestern North America. They are not, of course, observable in all of the footprints. However, whenever the soil or snow conditions are conducive to good print impressions, the characteristics described above are usually present. That fact is, in itself, excellent evidence that purported Bigfoot tracks are just that. They are not, obviously, the tracks made by foxes jumping or melted out bear tracks, as has been suggested.

I do not mean to imply that all "typical" Bigfoot prints are identical. That in itself would make them suspect. Besides the basic differences between the two common Northwest types as previously discussed, there are recognizable differences between prints left by different individuals, the most obvious being one of size. Most of the prints range between 14 and 18 inches in length and from 6 to 8 inches in width. Almost invariably, tracks smaller than 14 inches are found in company with other, larger prints.

The actual walking picture itself differs from the normal human arrangement in that the feet are ordinarily placed down one in front of another in an almost direct line. There is almost no toe-out at all, while the normal foot angle for humans is 30 to 32 degrees.

The length of stride for humans ordinarily runs from 20 to 40 inches with 27 inches considered normal for a walking adult. The giant prints often show a stride of 45 to 60 inches.

The actual size of the footprints is a little difficult to visualize from written descriptions or photographs. When seen in the ground or even when a plaster cast is examined, the overall proportions are most impressive. John Green quotes a shoe manufacturer as saying that a 15 inch Sasquatch print would require a size 21 long, but the width would have to be 13 sizes larger than the widest shoe made.

Equally as impressive as the size of the prints is the depth of the impressions in the soil. The prints invariably are sunk into the soil several times as far as human prints alongside. Dr. Maurice Tripp, geologist, made some engineering studies of the soil properties and depth of a Bigfoot print and concluded that the maker of the prints weighed in the neighborhood of 800 pounds.

The matter of the apparent weight of the giants was brought forcibly to my mind with our discovery of the very fresh tracks near Oroville, California. The creatures—two of them—had walked through the meadow only a short time before we had arrived. The heavy rain had stopped only a few minutes before our discovery of the tracks, yet they showed little evidence of having been rained upon. That means, of course, that the consistency of the mud in which they were made had changed very little before our arrival. The larger (15 inch) tracks were deeply imbedded in the mud. I was unable to match the depth of the prints even by jumping in the mud wearing heavy boots. I weigh just over 200 pounds.

Other Evidence

It is often said that we have no "hard" evidence relative to the ape-men. Because we cannot prove that certain hair and fecal samples are actually of Bigfoot origin, we must admit that we truly have no hard evidence—all of which is probably beside the point when we consider the following facts...

We do have photographs, casts, eye-witness descriptions and sketches of several hundred footprint impressions in mud, sand, dirt and snow. Those impressions exhibit, in the majority of cases, certain characteristics of foot shape and walking picture unlike that of man or any creature known to science. From the same localities, and often in conjunction with those tracks have come hundreds of eye-witness descriptions of encounters with giant ape-men. Even if we consider the unlikely possibility that all the alleged witnesses are liars or crackpots, we still have to explain those impressions in the soil and snow.

Something has to be making those tracks.

Along the same line, we can consider the matter of the hair and fecal evidence. Several samples of each have been analyzed in professional laboratories and found to be unidentifiable. Once again, something had to have produced those specimens. If they cannot be identified as having come from any known species, then it seems logical to conclude that they are from an unknown creature.

There have been a number of reports of possible Bigfoot excrement having been found and, in at least two cases, samples obtained for laboratory examination. Although the laboratory report in my file went into considerable detail, it boiled down to this final statement:

The feces belonged to some "unknown vegetarians." The lab described the specimen as dark grayish-olive in color and weighing 760 grams. The mass comprised almost completely of well-digested vegetable matter.

The general conclusion reached by the laboratory is as follows:

The evacuation is that of a large vegetarian animal, but shows characteristics not common to any cervid, moose or otherwise, all of which pass discrete beadlike pellets some times agglomerated into large masses, but never exhibiting the form presented by the sample. Fecal mass shows no resemblance to that of any species of bear examined for comparison. Nearest so far seen is that of the giant panda but the resemblance is only superficial.

The fecal mass that I found and photographed near the Oregon border appeared to be made up of a well-digested, slightly fibrous vegetable material. A number of examples of bear droppings found in the immediate vicinity were quite different in shape, color, consistency and odor.

Perhaps this scatalogical evidence is even more valuable than the many footprint casts and photographs because no one has yet suggested that the droppings have been faked!

As a well-known text on criminology points out, the examination and identification of hairs is a difficult and inexact science. It is not surprising then, to note that the few samples of possible Bigfoot hair so far collected have done little to substantiate the case.

I have so far had the opportunity to examine two samples of purported Bigfoot hair. One of those was collected by a guide near French Creek, Idaho. While fishing, he observed two large silver-grey humanoid creatures near the stream. He later found hairs on a bush nearby. John Green took the hairs to criminologist, Ray Pinker of Los Angeles State College for examination. The results of professor Pinker's examination were "inconclusive."

In 1971, John Dana and George Haas found some long, dark hairs on a log beside a trail of fresh Sasquatch prints in Northern California. I turned the hairs over to the Los Angeles County Sheriff's Department crime lab for examination. That laboratory, one of the finest in the nation, also reported the results of their examination as inconclusive.

The criminologists pointed out to me that the hairs had certain characteristics found only in human hair and certain characteristics found only in animal hair. Perhaps that tells us more than the criminologists realized.

A number of people claim to have come across beds that were possibly of Bigfoot origin. In most cases they described them as masses of moss, branches and grass, matted with feces and with a terrible urine-fecal odor. In some cases, crude weaving of the branches has been reported. There is also Albert Ostman's story of the woven blankets of his Sasquatch friends.

Such evidence is probably of little value unless the giants are actually observed in or near the beds. Simple weaving certainly should not be beyond the capabilities of the giants.

Many skeptics have pointed out that if a number of giants had been bounding through the forests of North America all these years, there would surely be remains found from time to time. In an interesting execution of reverse logic, paleontologists, both trained and self-appointed, have come to accept the absence of skeletal material as proof positive of the non-existence of any such creature as Bigfoot. Yet the same persons, if properly educated in primate evolution, will attribute a certain lack of knowledge about the evolution of forest apes, or of any jungle vertebrate for that matter, to the level of precipitation encountered in jungle forests. The bones are leached until they are quite fragile and are further dissolved in the acidic humus soil. These conditions of climate and soil, sadly, are found in almost every area where Bigfoot creatures are reported.

On at least two occasions, skeletal remains have been found that were probably of Bigfoot origin but, unfortunately, in both cases the bones have disappeared.

According to zoologist, Ivan Sanderson, he received information from a woman who stated that she and her husband uncovered a giant skeleton protruding from a bank of earth on Vancouver Island, She claims that the bones were sent to a museum in England, but Sanderson was unable to trace the remains.

From Nevada I have learned of the possible existence of the leg and foot bones of a giant man. The information that I received indicates that the bones were uncovered by a prospector about the turn of the century and kept as a display in a store window in a small town in Nevada. I have spoken to one old timer who vaguely remembers seeing them some years ago, but I cannot find what has become of them. The little old town in question is slowly fading and what population remains is made up primarily of people who have only lived there a few years.

Except for a specimen in the flesh, the most valuable piece of evidence of the existence of Bigfoot would be a good clear photograph. That we do not have, although Roger Patterson came fairly close. I have had the opportunity to examine Patterson's film and despite its technical photographic faults it is a fairly impressive piece of evidence.

Those few feet of movie film of a Bigfoot were taken October 20, 1967, at Bluff Creek, not far from Orleans, California. Patterson and his friend Bob Gimlin had planned to spend several weeks in the area to film some background material for a documentary on the subject. They had set up camp in Bluff Creek and were making daily horseback patrols up and down the canyon looking for tracks and filming the country. In late afternoon of that date they were riding upstream and just as they rounded a large pile of logs and debris both horses suddenly became frightened, reared and fell. Patterson, a former rodeo cowboy, suddenly found himself on foot. He went around to grasp the reins, and sighted a movement out of the corner of his eye. He turned to see a giant hairy humanoid creature running up the sandbank from the stream bed.

Patterson grabbed his camera, turned it on and gave chase. Upon reaching the top of the sandbank Patterson stopped, planted his feet firmly and got a few feet of fairly clear film.

The creature at first moved off at a smooth trot, but then apparently caught the sound of the camera and turned head and shoulders to look at Patterson. She then speeded up, moving into the forest and up a steep bank where she disappeared. Gimlin started to give chase, but Patterson, armed only with the camera, called him back, not really wanting to be left alone under those circumstances. They then went to work casting the tracks before returning to civilization with the films.

After viewing the film several times, at various speeds and in stills, I can describe the creature in the following way; a bipedal primate of extremely massive proportions, covered with dark hair from head to foot, long, thick arms, large head with a definite slope to the forehead and with little or no neck. It was apparently a female with large pendulous breasts. Sounds about like what people have been describing all along doesn't it?

There were four points about the film that seemed most important.

The massiveness of the creature. I suppose all of us had through the years of investigation formed a mental picture of the creatures based upon eye-witness descriptions. Nevertheless, the bulk of the giant is surprising. The broad, thickset body, the powerful thighs and thick buttocks are very impressive.

The specimen in the film is "hairier" than I had expected, and the hair covering is more complete, with only the bottoms of the feet and the area around the eyes visibly free of hair. Patterson stated that the coloring was brown, fairly dark underneath, lighter on the tips, but in the film it appears nearly black.

Another noticeable feature was the smooth, gliding gait. I feel that the primary difference between the gait of man and the creature in the film is the lack of vertical movement or bobbing in the giant. The difference is apparently caused by the Bigfoot running with bent knees.

The only time the knees seem to straighten out is as they are extended forward. When the weight is placed on the foot, the knee is definitely bent, resulting in a smooth, gliding gait.

Most of us viewing the film received the distinct impression that the creature was not really frightened. Although she was leaving the scene at some speed, you get the feeling that she would be capable of far greater speed. There is definitely no panic flight involved.

Apparently Patterson's camera was not correctly focused as the details most needed are simply not visible. The facial features cannot be seen clearly although there is definitely a face, rather than an animal-like snout. The hands appear to be carried with curved fingers, like a scoop. The skin, where it shows around the eyes appears shiny black and in fact seems to be reflecting some sunlight.

A little over a week after the film was taken, Bob Titmus made a series of 10 plaster casts of the footprints at the scene. He noted the subtle yet important differences from one print to another, Those differences more than any other point, convinced Titmus of the authenticity of the tracks, Titmus followed the tracks up the side of the mountain to a spot above and within view of where the pictures were taken. It appeared to Titmus that the creature sat down and watched Patterson and Gimlin examining the tracks.

Knowing the track length (14½ inches), and using the full foot as seen in some frames of the picture, it is possible to determine the height of the creature quite closely. Using that method, it has been determined that she was just under 7 feet tall. This is on the bottom of the scale of reported Bigfoot sightings which range all the way to 10 feet and more. That height seems reasonable considering the size of the footprints which are also relatively small for Bigfoot prints.

The general proportions of Patterson's Bigfoot appear, except for their bulk, to be quite human-like until closer examination is made. Actually, the body is longer in proportion to overall height than is normal for man. The great bulk of the torso creates the illusion that it is short, but measurements prove otherwise.

That disproportionate torso length also fools the eye in relation to the arm length. The arm spread is almost 9 feet, a full 2 feet greater than her height in running posture.

Compared to man, the head is disproportionately large, even for the huge body on which it rests. Because of the hair, it is difficult to tell just how large the neck is or, for that matter, whether or not there is a neck. At the place in the area between the head and the shoulders, in other words where the neck "belongs" the measurement appears to be about equal to a man's chest.

Although relatively short, the legs are more man-like than ape-like. They are powerfully developed and the buttocks area is thick, as in a powerful, muscular man.

As John Green points out, there is no reason to assume that this is a typical Bigfoot figure or to assume that there is any less variation among such creatures than there is among individuals of species *homo sapiens*.

This much can be said for the Patterson film: he was lucky, very lucky, indeed. Although it was 3:30 in the afternoon, he just happened to be in a portion of the canyon that is wider than most, allowing in the afternoon sunlight.

He also had a series of fortunate circumstances that allowed him to come upon the giant undetected. To begin with, the creature was apparently crouched at the stream where the sound of the horses hooves on the rocky stream bed were not heard. The wind was blowing downstream toward Patterson and Gimlin, again giving them an unusual opportunity to get quite close before being detected. Perhaps most important of all was a great fallen tree and the pile of flood debris that shut them off from view of the giant. I wonder how long it will be before any of us are again so fortunate?

The Patterson film has had a most interesting history. Patterson, no doubt felt he had a piece of film that would prove to be of great value to science. He also probably believed that he and Gimlin would make a good deal of money from it. Neither assumption proved entirely correct.

The film did not exactly take the scientific world by storm. He had great difficulty getting the American scientists to view it, and none of them took the time to study it carefully.

It was not until 1971 that serious scientific study of the film was made and that was by British and Russian experts. In that year Rene Dahinden took a copy of the film to Europe.

In England, a bio-chemical study was made by Dr. D.W. Grieve. He points out that the speed at which the film was exposed is most critical. If it was taken at 24 frames per second, then the gait could have been that of a man. If set at 16-18 fps then it would be impossible for a normal human being to duplicate the walking pattern. Patterson stated that he ordinarily used 24 fps, but after the encounter, found the camera set at 18 fps. He did not know when it was changed. Dr. Grieve commented that the film would have been difficult to fake.

It is my understanding that a copy is still under study by the Russian experts and that their preliminary comments have been favorable to the authenticity of the film.

In evaluating the possibility of a hoax here, there are several points to be considered. John Green tells me that the film was examined by moving picture experts in Hollywood. They commented that there is definitely no trick photography involved. The Bigfoot thing was not added in the laboratory.

If the picture is fake, then either Patterson was involved in the deception or someone else managed to fool him quite successfully.

Whatever it was that ran along the stream bank in front of Patterson's camera had to be either a Bigfoot, a man in disguise or a mechanical gadget of some sort. It seems quite unlikely that it was a man in an ape suit for the following reasons: (a) the great size. I have been to the scene and judging by the background and foreground material, the size as estimated by Patterson seems reasonable to me; (b) Next is the matter of the gait. I have never seen a human's legs operate in just that manner. (c) The "hang" of the arms. The giant's shoulders are extremely broad and if that had been accomplished by the use of padding, the arm and shoulder relationship would appear unnatural. Shoulders can be widened, but the arms cannot be moved outward. In the film the arms appear to be in a normal relationship to the shoulders.

If we wish to believe that the object in the film is a mechanical device of some sort, then we will have to admit that it was a very poor investment for someone. To create such a remarkable machine would require the expenditure of considerable sums of money. Either Patterson was involved in the hoax or he was not. There is no evidence that he had either the technical or the financial resources at his disposal to create such a thing. If he is not involved, then someone went to a great deal of bother and expense to play a trick on Patterson. To do so required transporting the "thing" up Bluff Creek and setting it in motion at just the time and place where Patterson and Gimlin would ride upon the scene. Also the pranksters must have taken it for granted that neither Patterson or Gimlin would use their rifles.

Keep in mind also that professional taxidermist and experienced Bigfooter Bob Titmus took a number of casts of prints at the scene. He was absolutely convinced of their authenticity.

Incredibly, after nine years, the only piece of important photographic evidence we have, remains a matter of great controversy. It is most certainly only a matter of time before other, and hopefully, better pictures are made. There are a number of well-equipped and dedicated researchers working nearly full time in an attempt to accomplish that very thing. In the meantime, Patterson's few feet of shaky, poorly-focused movie film may well be one of the most important strips of film ever exposed.

Supporting Evidence

Reports of sounds and odors are hardly the type of evidence to prove or disprove the existence of the giants. Nevertheless they are an important part of the whole picture and in some ways are matters of some significance, as we shall see.

Those unfamiliar with life in the forests are often misled by sounds they hear in the wild. A couple of coyotes a half mile away can sound to the tenderfoot like a whole pack just a few feet away. The scream of a cougar sounds exactly like a woman in great pain. The "blow" of an alarmed deer is often not recognized at all by those unfamiliar with the woods. But as unreliable as sounds can be, the fact that certain sounds are repeatedly reported in conjunction with other Bigfoot activity is important.

Although various types of screams, growls, chattering and grunts have been mentioned at one time or another, one sound is most commonly reported. It is described as a high-pitched, whistling scream.

Among investigators, both George Haas and Nick Campbell have heard and described the screams. Nick has attempted to describe the sound he heard in February 1974, but admits that it is really impossible to either imitate or describe. He says that if you can imagine the ridiculous combination of a screech owl, a howling coyote and a trumpeting elephant you might get the picture. Of the five series of screams he heard one night near his camp, each started low and ended in a very high pitch.

Albert Ostman claimed his captors "spoke" to each other.

He stated that most of it just sounded like jabbering of some sort, but he did clearly recall the "word" *soka-soka*. That is the sound made by the female when she attempted to prevent him from fleeing from the giants.

A monkey-like chatter has been reported in a

number of incidents. Homer Stickly distinctly heard a chattering on his ranch during the time that the creatures were frequenting the area.

The matter of odors is a particularly interesting one in our study of the giants. In a great many reports wherein the creatures are observed at close range, an over-powering stench is mentioned, yet in other, equally close encounters no mention is made of odor.

Patterson mentioned the stench and described it as the odor of a wet dog that had rolled in excrement.

In some accounts, the odor is the most clearly-remembered element of the sighting. Why some observers report no odor at all is interesting. Possibly fear on the part of the observer is the explanation. It seems odd, however, that many witnesses who can remember quite a number of other details of the incident, would fail to recall the stench, if one existed.

This brings to mind the possibility that the giants are equipped with musk glands. In fact, several witnesses have reported the odor as a strong, musky one. It is possible that the giants can control the glands, to emit the odor at will as in the skunk. Possibly the glands operate automatically when the creature is badly frightened.

Behavior

A discussion of Bigfoot behavior is important for several reasons. Perhaps most important is the fact that if many of the alleged sightings were in fact tall-tales, then some of the storytellers would most likely get carried away and describe the giants doing things that would, in fact, be impossible. Actually, none of the activities so far described appear to be impossible or even improbable for a giant, powerful, bipedal primate.

Because, in only a very few cases, have the giants been observed without their knowledge, most of our reports concern their reactions to man.

Most common of those reactions, obviously, is flight.

Seldom does that appear to be panic flight, but rather a hurried, controlled exit. Interestingly, in a certain percentage of cases, these supposedly shy and retiring creatures seem quite unconcerned with the presence of man. Perhaps even more interesting are the surprising number of cases in which the creatures seem to intentionally approach man for one reason or another.

One example is the case of a Victorville, California couple who told me of an incident that had occurred in 1965. They were picnicking at the mouth of the Deep creek, near Hesperia, California and were sitting around the campfire just after dark. The husband noted what he thought to be the shining eyes of an owl in a tree nearby. He was just thinking to himself that it must be a very large owl, due to the distance between the eyes, when he remembered there were no trees in the immediate area. He grabbed his wife by the arm and said "come on, we're leaving..." As the they hurried toward his pickup truck parked nearby, they looked behind them and observed a tall, shadowy figure following them. It appeared to be only following and kept a good distance behind them. They reached the truck, jumped in and sped away, just as the creature reached the edge of the roadway.

From the brief glimpse they got in the headlights, they described it in the following way. "...about 8 feet tall, heavily built with a head like a football helmet. Its eyes shone yellow green."

The actions of the beast in this incident are those of

a curious, rather than an aggressive creature. Perhaps it was the odor of roasting wieners that had attracted it, or perhaps the sound of the portable radio.

One investigator feels that some of the giant's actions in relation to humans might be attributed to a sense of humor on their part. Is it possible that they are just sufficiently man-like to enjoy a good joke? What could be funnier than the reactions of the frightened humans upon encountering one of the monsters? Certainly in some reports they would appear to be intentionally exposing their presence without any other logical explanation possible.

We have a report from a Dallas, Oregon woman who stated that she was sitting on her front porch when two of the giants walked across a field in front of her house in broad daylight.

They seemed to pay no attention to her or to her two dogs. The dogs stayed on the porch barking and made no move to chase the ape-men. There were trees just beyond the edge of the field and the giants could have easily traveled approximately the same route without being seen, by merely remaining within the tree cover. Why they chose not to do so is an intriguing question.

We have a number of cases in our files in which the ape-men have exhibited extreme curiosity concerning humans and their activities. A typical example is the case of Mrs. Louise Baxter of Skamania, Washington. On August 19,1970, she got out of her car to check to see if she had a flat tire. She states that as she bent over to check one of the tires, she suddenly felt as if she was being watched.

She says, "without looking up, I glanced toward the wooded area beside the road and looked straight into the face of the biggest creature I have ever seen."

The creature was coconut brown and shaggy and dirty-looking.

It had one huge fist up to its mouth. The mouth was partly open and I saw a row of large square teeth. The head was big and seemed to set right onto the shoulders. The ears were not visible due to the long hair on the head. It seemed the hair was about 2 inches long on its head.

It had a jutted chin and a receding forehead. The nose and upper lip were less hairy and the nose was wide with big nostrils. The eyes were the most outstanding as they were amber color and seemed to glow like an animal's eyes at night when car lights catch them.

"It seemed to be eating, as the left fist was up toward the mouth as though it had something in it. I screamed or hollered but whether I made any noise I can't tell, I was so terrified. I know it didn't move while I looked. I don't remember how I got back in the car or how I started it. As I pulled out, I could see it still standing there, all 10 or 12 feet of him."

There are also quite a number of cases in which the giants appear to be more than curious, although just what their actions indicate remains a mystery. For instance, we have several reports of campers and trailers or cars being violently shaken by the ape-men. One example is the report made by Benjamin Wilder in September 1964.

Wilder was asleep in his car near Blue Lake, California, when he was awakened by what he thought was an earthquake. He turned on his flashlight and was startled to find a large animal standing by the driver's door. He shouted, but the creature continued shaking the car. Wilder then sounded the horn and the animal ran off on two legs, making noises like a hog.

The elusiveness of the Sasquatch is further questioned when we note the number of cases in which they approach homes, barns, camps or vehicles that are occupied by humans. In several cases they have been observed reaching into tents or through the windows of homes or vehicles.

Harry Squiness of Anaheim Lake, B.C., told John Green of such an incident that occurred in the early fall of 1962. He was camping with his family in a tent and one night just before he dozed off, he saw a head and forearm come in through the tent flap. It was a monkey-like face, but on a head larger than a man's and the arm was covered with long dark hair.

Mr. Squiness grabbed for his gun and the creature left the tent, As the witness stepped out, he saw four creatures that had been lying down, get up and walk slowly away. All were about 8 feet tall. He believes that the baby's crying may have attracted the giants.

Statistically, we note an interesting situation in regard to the Sasquatch "approaches." In approximately three out of four cases in which the giants show no fear, the human observers are either women or children. In the vast majority of those cases where the observers are men, they are unarmed.

Assuming the giants to be generally shy, retiring creatures, it is always surprising to receive reports wherein their actions are decidedly at variance with their normal, elusive behavior. In going over the files we find a surprising number of instances in which they have performed overt acts of mischief (or anger).

The Bluff Creek incidents of 1958 are excellent

examples.

Drums of diesel oil were moved around, steel culverts were thrown into ravines, and trailers overturned. These are hardly the acts of wild creatures instinctively trying to avoid contact with civilization. If such mischief seems surprisingly "non-animal" in nature, we can recall the behavior of chimps in the zoo. Perhaps mischievous and sometimes destructive behavior is characteristic of the primates.

Still other examples of Bigfoot behavior are even more surprising. We have two separate reports in which the giants have run alongside moving vehicles as if pacing them. Then, there is the 1973 report from Antelope Valley California in which the ape-men pursued a pickup truck. Stranger still, we have two reports, neither of which has been thoroughly investigated, in which injured hunters have been carried to safety by the giants.

As in all other facets of the ape-man mystery, the matter of behavior is fascinating and often unexplainable. There seem to be no elements of standard behavior that can be attributed to the giants. Perhaps the odd and unusual behavior is simply further proof of the man-like qualities of Bigfoot. It is a general rule of zoology that the higher the level of intelligence, the less standardized the habit patterns tend to be.

Eating Habits

In the earlier years of the investigation we believed the giants were strictly vegetarians. The only two specimens of probable Bigfoot feces so far examined in a proper laboratory have proven to be made up entirely of vegetable matter. It also seems obvious that the Bigfoot/ Sasquatch of the Northwest represent a race of surviving gigantopithecus, a supposedly extinct ape-man, who was apparently a vegetarian.

In recent years we have received a sufficient number of reports of the giants eating meat or fish to justify belief in their omnivorous habits. It also adds some credence to claims by some Indian tribes that the giants are meat-eaters.

Our information relating to Sasquatch foods indicates they have most often been observed eating berries. Other foods, in order of the frequency of reports are as follows: roots, tree leaves or buds, water plants, deer, garbage, fish, sheep, dogs and rodents.

There have been a number of other incidents in which the ape-men have been observed stalking or chasing deer, cattle, horses, sheep or dogs. There can be little doubt that deer form a part of their diet, although they may have some difficulty in capturing full-grown deer. It also appears that they sometimes depend upon man for assistance in supplying a venison meal.

Gary Joanis of Eugene, Oregon reported that in 1957 while he and a friend, Jim Newell, were hunting, he lost a deer to one of the giants. He stated they were hunting at Wanoga Butte, southwest of Bend when the unusual incident occurred. Joanis said the deer had entered a clearing acting as if something was following it and did not notice him at all. He shot it, but before he could reach the carcass, a 9 foot hairy giant emerged from the forest, gathered it under one arm and ran off, making a whistling scream. Joanis fired several shots at the creature with his 30.06 and believes he hit it, but did not attempt to follow it into the forest.

It may be that the giants have found rural highways to

be convenient places to obtain animals struck by vehicles. A surprisingly large percentage of sightings take place on roads and in several instances the giants appeared to be eating at a deer carcass.

Summary of Evidence

In reading the more detailed sighting reports, the reader will have noted certain common denominators, certain elements that are found in the vast majority of alleged sightings. Over and over again, the great size, hairiness and stench of the creatures is mentioned. Great size is mentioned in all but a tiny percentage of cases. Hairiness in all cases. Stench was mentioned in over half of the incidents where the observer was close to the creature or creatures.

The constant repetition of those elements in the reports is still another strong argument for the existence of the ape-men. It would seem logical to assume that if any great number of alleged witnesses were actually lying or hallucinating, there would be some glaring exceptions in the descriptions. The fact that there are not is, in my opinion, most significant.

Additional examples of the uniformity of descriptions are readily available. For example, in every case where the neck is mentioned it is described as very short or non-existent.

In every instance where facial features are mentioned they are described as ape-like or words to that effect. The nose is invariably described as flat or ape-like.

In no case have the giants been described as using tools or weapons. In only one case has any type of clothing been mentioned and that by a very young, frightened witness.

In all cases where the running gait of the creatures is mentioned it is described as rapid, agile or smooth, never as clumsy or lumbering. There are repeated references to exaggerated arm-swinging.

In most night sightings, where some light shined on the monster, reflecting or glowing eyes are mentioned.

Descriptions of hair color vary widely, but are within the known range of variations known to other primates, including man. The colors reported are black, brown, grey, silver-tipped, white, reddish-brown and yellow-brown.

Footprints left by the Northwest giants appear to have been made by feet logically adapted to use by a biped of enormous weight.

It seems likely that anyone with sufficient imagination to dream up an alleged Bigfoot encounter might also be inclined to throw in a few details that would not fit our picture. The more thoroughly we study the files, the more obvious it becomes that all or certainly the vast majority of the witnesses are describing or trying to describe just what they actually did see—a giant ape-men.

It should be obvious to the reader by now that even without live specimen or a carcass, we have sufficient evidence to substantiate belief in the existence of the monster-men of the Northwest woods. Additionally, our evidence is now sufficient to form a reasonably clear picture of their physical description. That description is defined in some detail in Chapter 3.

The reader should keep in mind that in this chapter we have been dealing specifically with the Bigfoot/Sasquatch of the Northwest. There are obviously other "man-things" in North America and the information we have concerning them will be discussed in the following chapter.

Chapter 7
Those "Other Things"

As described in an earlier chapter, monster hunters have been forced to face a disturbing fact: there is, in addition to the Sasquatch, several other varieties of man-monsters roaming the backwoods of North America. The total volume of evidence collected relative to these "other" creatures is not nearly so great as that accumulated in Bigfoot/Sasquatch research, but it is sufficient to demonstrate that they differ in important ways from the giants of the Northwest.

The relative scarcity of accumulated data may well be more the result of a lack of investigative effort, than a lack of available information. To my knowledge, the only active investigators who have applied their efforts to areas outside the Northwest are Michael Bershod, Loren Coleman and the late Gary Williamson. Bershod, like most researchers in this field has only limited time to devote to the subject and has pretty-well limited his efforts to investigating reports in his home area of Maryland. Coleman has recently moved to the West Coast and the excellent work being done by Gary Williamson came to a tragic end with his death in an automobile accident.

It is interesting and perhaps significant to note that the bulk of the investigation in the Midwest, South and East has been carried on by representatives of various UFO study groups. Stan Gordon's MUFON group in Pennsylvania has perhaps made the most important contribution.

It would be a gross understatement to admit that the picture is still unclear relative to these other apemen. On the one hand we have what at first appear to be Bigfoot reports emanating from nearly every state. On the other hand, we find that a large percentage of reports originating outside the Northwest contain information foreign to the more "typical" Northwest incidents.

Like it or not, we must face the following facts relative to sightings throughout the country. A sizable percentage of footprints found in conjunction with apeman sightings are of a type (or types) entirely different than the well-known giant tracks of the Northwest. Some of the creatures described exhibit notably different physical characteristics than those common to the Sasquatch.

Some of the behavioral characteristics and other circumstances of these reports show great variation from typical Sasquatch/Bigfoot encounters.

Pertaining to the apparent UFO involvement in some cases, if we are going to be really objective we cannot, unfortunately, ignore some evidence simply because we don't like it or because it seems "unbelievable."

It would be convenient to be able to clearly define the habitat ranges of the various types of man-monsters in North America. Unfortunately, there are enough exceptions to each case to weaken any distribution theory so far advanced.

We can say, however, that the majority of the 4-toed prints have been found in the arid or semi-arid regions of the West and Southwest. The majority of the 3-toed prints have been reported from the Mississippi River, east. Most reports of the dwarf ape-men have come from the western portion of the country.

If all those odd and unusual "whatchamacallits" are indeed indigenous to North America, then they must have evolved specific characteristics of survival fitting them for certain types of habitat. On the other hand, if, as a growing number of researchers are beginning to suspect, some of them have been transported here from outer space, then any efforts to define distribution patterns may be useless.

The Abominable Sandman

The most unlikely locale imaginable as a stomping ground for a giant primate would seem to be the arid wasteland of the Borrego Badlands of Southern California. Nevertheless, that dry, barren, seemingly lifeless region has, through the years, produced a surprising number of reports that seem to be describing creatures similar in some ways to the giants of the damp, cold Northwest rain forests.

The Legend of Dead Man's Hole is a gruesome tale originating in an area now known as Blair Valley at the west end of the Borrego Badlands. In 1858, an unidentified prospector was killed there; some stories say he was found decapitated. Another victim was killed there in 1858, although the circumstances of the killing are not clear. In 1922, rancher Will Blair was found dead there with large finger marks on his neck. His body appeared to have been dragged some distance. That same year, an Indian girl named Belita was killed at Dead Man's Hole. She had been strangled and her body was badly crumpled.

Only a few months after the killing of the Indian girl, two San Diego men, Ed Dean and Charles Cox, claimed to have shot and killed an ape-man at Dead Man's Hole.

It is interesting to note that with only four reports in our files in which an ape-man has been shot and killed, two of the reports originate in the Borrego area.

An old newspaper article from 1880 describes the killing of a gorilla-like animal by a prospector. The incident is supposed to have occurred near Warner's Springs, which is in the foothills northwest of the Badlands.

In 1964, *Desert Magazine* published an article entitled "Abominable Sandman of Borrego." The article described tracks found by a retired army officer who was prospecting in the south part of the Badlands. Photos accompanying the article showed broad, indistinct footprint impressions in the dry, sandy soil. The number and shape of the toes was not clearly discernible in the photograph. The over-all proportions of the footprints appear to be similar to the 4-toed tracks we found near Alpine in 1972. Alpine is just over the mountains to the west of the Borrego Desert.

The most detailed information from the Borrego area concerns the sighting by the Los Angeles man who reported encountering several white, hairy giants there in 1939. Rich Grumly of the California Bigfoot Organization put me in touch with the witness in 1972. Rich tells me that he first heard the story from him in 1961, which is a matter of some importance, as we shall see.

The more important details of the interview are as follows...

When and where did the incident occur?

Witness: In the late fall of 1939, near a place called Wolf's Head Pass, on the California-Arizona border.

Would you describe the terrain please?

Witness:It's what you would call desert country— not sand dunes, but desert hills and dry washes.

Were you alone and what were you doing out there?

Witness: I was alone except for my burro and I was prospecting.

Would you tell me what happened please?

Witness: I had built a shelter in a depression in the canyon wall and covered it with some driftwood and brush, because the nights were pretty cold. The burro and I were inside the shelter and I had built a fire at the entrance. During the night, the burro made a big fuss and woke me up. Then I noticed the thing trying to get past the fire to where I was.

Please describe the "thing."

Witness: It was white all over, with long hair. It had a face more like a man than an animal.

How large was it?

Witness: It was kind of squatted down all the time I saw it, but I think if it had stood up it would be about seven feet tall and 300 pounds or more.

Why was it squatting down?

Witness: It was crouching down to get into the opening in the shelter. It wanted to get to me real bad, but it seemed to be afraid of the fire. All I had was a

145

.38 pistol so I did not want to shoot at it. I built up the fire some more and that seemed to drive it off. When it backed up I noticed several more like him out there in the dark—4 or 5 maybe.

What can you tell me about its features?

Witness: *I couldn't see too much because of the hair all over his face, and the only light was the campfire. His eyes glowed red in the firelight and he had fangs. I could see his teeth when he growled at me. Sort of a low growl.*

Did he make any other noise, or did any of the others?

Witness: *He just growled and that is the only noise I heard. I couldn't see the others very well because they were out in the dark. I don't think they made any noise.*

Did you notice any odor?

Witness: *I don't remember any, but I was pretty scared at the time and there may have been lots of things that I didn't remember.*

What finally happened?

Witness: *I kept throwing wood on the fire until I ran out of it, but by that time they had all disappeared.*

What do you think they were?

Witness: *Some kind of ape, but I know there aren't supposed to be any apes in North America.*

As I interviewed the witness, I observed that he perspired profusely and exhibited other signs of nervousness, as if he was re-living an incident that had been more than a little frightening. Keep in mind that the incident occurred 30 years before he related it to me, although he remembered some details, but not so many as to make me suspicious. It seems reasonable that after that many years, only certain points would be clearly remembered. Glowing red eyes, fangs and a low growl seem to me the very type of thing most likely to be remembered. As he pointed out, he had been 19 at the time and very frightened. In attempting to determine the authenticity of this tale, I believe it is important that the first time he mentioned it to anyone had been in 1961, when he related it to Rich. It is only very recently that such details as glowing red eyes and white fur have been mentioned in print.

In an earlier chapter, I have described the circumstances surrounding the sightings of the "big monkeys" by the doctor in Alpine, San Diego County. The footprints we observed in two locations near Alpine were quite broad at the front of the foot, tapering to a pointed heel. There were just four toes. Edward Woods, chief of the Viejas Indian Reservation near Alpine told us of several incidents in which tribal members had encountered large "apes" on or near the reservation.

Joel Hurd uncovered numerous old rumors and local legends of monsters in the area of Eastern San Diego County. One of those, the "Legend of the Japatul Valley Monster," described the killing of cattle by "giant apes."

A man named Harold Lancaster claims to have seen an ape-man east of Borrego Springs in July 1968. Other reports, many of them little more than vague rumors, reach us from time to time, from that desert area.

It seems almost certain, then, that a race of ape-men inhabit the arid and semi-arid wastelands of extreme Southern California. The creatures are probably somewhat smaller than the giants of the Northwest, and they obviously have very odd-shaped, 4-toed feet.

How a race of giant primates manage to find sufficient sustenance to survive in that forbidding land is a mystery in itself. It is my personal belief that they actually make their home in the range of mountains separating the Borrego Desert from the rest of San Diego County. Those mountains would afford some vegetation, water and wildlife not available on the desert side. On the western side of the mountains there are many ranches and at the higher elevations, some fruit orchards. The reports of their raiding of ranches and orchards may be proof that they do, at times, find survival difficult.

Some researchers have pointed out that the Superstition Mountains in the Borrego Badlands might well be home base of the giants. Some geologists believe that mountain range contains vast underground caverns and water, although no cavern openings have yet been found. Investigator, Lee Trippett, pointed out years ago that most Bigfoot reports originate in areas where caves or volcanic tubes are common.

The Dwarf Ape-Men

Of the several types of man-monsters apparently inhabiting our continent, the dwarf type has received least publicity. They are perhaps the most mysterious of all. Everything about them seems unreal and yet, once again, we have some pretty substantial evidence to justify belief in their existence. I will not believe that those tiny footprints I found on two separate occasions in Northern California were the tracks of human children, nor were they the tracks of any known animal.

Those footprints were found in out-of-the-way places under very interesting circumstances. Whatever made those tracks possesses feet smaller than those of an adult human, with a foot shape totally different than any I have ever seen on a human. The heels tapered to a definite point and the toes were evenly arranged in a straight line. Many researchers have pointed out that nearly every Indian tribe in the Northwest has legends concerning the giants. Those old tribal tales correspond with the information from modern reports in nearly every detail. What many of those same investigators apparently don't realize is that Indian legends contain at least as many references to "the Little People."

Ella E. Clark, in her *Indian Legends of the Northern Rockies*, describes many of those old stories told by the Indians of Montana, Idaho, Wyoming, and Eastern Washington.

According to the Nez Perce, the "Little People" still live in the mountains and have, on occasion, kidnapped Indian children.

An early pioneer in the Wind River country of Wyoming claimed to have come upon a series of crude stone dwellings high among the rocks near the source of Muddy Creek. The local Indians explained to him that the dwellings had been made by the Ninnimbe or little demons.

Both the Shoshoni and Bannock tribes tell stories of cannibal dwarfs that formerly lived in the Owyhee range and the Salmon River country of Idaho. The Indians claim they were seldom seen until dusk.

Old Arapahos say that a race of 3-foot-tall, dark skinned, "people" used to live in caves in the mountains.

Old Spokane and Couer D'Alene Indians relate tales of the 3-foot-tall "Little People." They apparently lived high in the mountains and were nocturnal in habits. Some stories mention the dwarfs wearing brown suits with pointed caps, possibly referring to brown fur covering and a pointed head similar to that of the Bigfoot creatures. Other stories described the dwarfs as red or dressed in red. That coloring description will become significant when we look into the matter of the "Little Red Men of The Delta." White men have been reporting encounters with small hairy, man-like creatures for many, many years.

The earliest published record was found by Gordon Strassenburgh in the Library of Congress. The story was published by the Dorchester County, Maryland, *Aurora*, August 27, 1838. It described a creature resembling a 7- or 8-year old child, covered entirely with black hair. When pursued, the creature fled at great speed and emitted a whistling sound. According to the report, a number of people had encountered the creature, but no one had been able to capture it.

The *Philadelphia Saturday Courier*, on December 28, 1839, carried a report from Michigan City, Indiana describing a "wild child" frequently seen near Fish Lake. The creature was 4-feet-tall, covered with chestnut hair. It was said that it "ran with great velocity and made frightful and hideous yells." When pursued, it would plunge into the lake and swim at great speed.

Strangely, most Indian legends concerning the dwarfs are found in the Northern and Northwestern part of the country, while most of the recent reports have come from the Mississippi Valley with its thousands of square miles of bottomlands. Rural folk who live in the lowland forested areas along the great river sometimes speak of the "Little Red Men of the Trees" or the "Swamp Apes." In the deep South, we hear the term Woolybooger used by the country people. That name is sometimes used in reference to a giant hairy ape-man and sometimes is meant to describe the "Monkey-Men" or "Little Red Men" who live back in the bayous. Are these no more than rural folk tales? People who live in the backwoods of Mississippi, Kentucky, Arkansas, Southern Illinois, Missouri and Tennessee speak seriously of the matter. There are a number of published accounts to substantiate the tales.

In the early 1940s, a number of residents of Southern Illinois reported sighting an animal "something like a baboon." In the summer of 1941, a minister reported that a creature of that description had jumped out of a tree and approached him while he was squirrel hunting near Mt. Vernon. He drove the creature off by striking it with his rifle barrel.

Other reports from nearby rural districts described the terrifying screams of the beast or beasts. A farmer near Bonnie reported his dog killed by the "ape." The creatures were usually described as bipedal and extremely agile. A man driving near the Big Muddy River in Jackson County claimed to have seen one bound across the road with 20-foot leaps.

James Meacham reported that while hunting near Jackson, Tennessee in 1951, he shot at a reddish-orange "ape." He stated that the creature had no tail, but was climbing in the trees like a monkey. He fired 14 shots at it with his .22 and is certain that some of the shots struck the creature, but without noticeable effect.

Zoologist Ivan Sanderson reported that his research had turned up reports of the Little Red Men of the Delta. He said they were described as about the size of a 10-year-old child, and that they can climb like monkeys and also spend a lot of time in the water.

Most Bigfoot researchers occasionally come across stories about children who claim to have played in the woods with the "monkeys." A number of people who have grown up in the rural districts of the Northwest will admit, privately, that as children they often played with little furry man-like creatures in the forest near their homes. Most often, they had reported their activities to their parents and were either ignored or lectured on the subject of truthfulness. Most often, those same informants have assumed that the creatures were simply the young of the Sasquatch. Upon further questioning, it becomes clear in many cases that the creatures in question were far too small to have been the young of the giant ape-men.

The reports of the dwarf ape-men are far less common than are the reports of sightings of the giants. That fact may or may not indicate a much greater rarity on the part of the small creatures. The vast majority of reports of the dwarfs relate to sightings, while nearly half of the giant reports concern footprints. It is most likely that the small tracks often go unnoticed or are mistaken for the footprints of children. Also, the weight of the creatures is probably not sufficient to leave identifiable impressions.

As might be expected, the dwarf ape-men appear to be even more shy than the giants. Living as they do in the heavily forested canyons or bayous they could conceivably be quite numerous and yet be seldom encountered by man.

We cannot merely ignore the reports because they are less common than sightings of the giants. Every year or so, a new report or a series of reports comes to us describing sightings of the dwarfs. Except for the quantity, there is no more reason to doubt those accounts than the reports of the giants.

Uno Heckkila, of Floodwood, Minnesota, made such a report in 1968. He claimed that on November 12, while hunting west of Duluth, he observed a 4½-foot-tall creature jump down from a tree and walk into the woods, upright.

A very similar report was made by Nathan Russell near Truman, Arkansas, in February 1969. I have noticed with considerable interest that some Bigfoot researchers tend to ignore the reports of the dwarf ape-men. Others are satisfied with the explanation that they are merely the young of the giants.

Some skeptics have pointed out that with little or no evidence, we are going out on a limb somewhat, even considering the possibility of the existence of the dwarfs. I disagree.

First, the matter of the Indian legends must be considered. The same tribes whose descriptions of the giants tally perfectly with what we now know of them, also repeatedly mention the dwarfs. If those tribal legends have proven so reliable on the one hand, it is reasonable to assume reliability on the other. Some of the old Indians who know tribal history claim the Little People were killed off by the white man. But were they? There are a great many people who have spent their lives in the bayou country of the Mississippi Valley who know of the Little Red Men of the Delta.

Additional confirmation is found in the fact that stories of small, furry, man-like creatures have come from many other parts of the world. Particularly important is the fact that the descriptions of the creatures from those other areas agree in important details with the descriptions of our dwarf ape-men.

Natives in some parts of South America speak of the Dwendi, a small man-like creature covered with brown or reddish-brown fur and with a mane down the head and back. The Dwendi's are said to be very curious about humans and their activities, but are also extremely shy and apparently quite harmless to humans. In some regions they are known to carry off dogs. Their footprints are tiny and almost like prints of human child except for the pointed heels.

Descriptions of similar creatures have come from many areas of Africa and Asia. Such reports almost invariably originate in areas of dense rain forest.

Considering the difficulty we have had gathering evidence of the existence of the giants, it seems none too surprising that so little is known of the dwarfs. The most advanced and civilized nation on earth has developed on the continent of North America in the last 200 years. Amidst all that progress, a race, or races, of giant ape-men have managed to avoid man to the extent that they are even today officially "non-existent." Does it seem unreasonable then, to assume that a race of dwarf ape-men, living in the deepest canyons and most impenetrable forests could have eluded man also.

The 3-Toed Man-Monsters

This matter of the 3-toed giants slipped up on us and caught us all by surprise. By "us," I mean, of course, the Bigfoot buffs, Sasquatch seekers, monster hunters or whatever name you care to attach to the strange type of individual who is willing to spend his time in pursuit of "legendary" ape-men.

I was quite surprised to learn of ape-man reports

from the South, the Midwest, and the East. The newsclippings seemed to describe something like the Northwest Sasquatch, and it was the locale that seemed extraordinary. As time went by, we began to wonder if the reports were speaking of nothing more than a displaced Bigfoot. We noted some slight discrepancies in physical description and then we began to hear of the 3-toed footprints.

I have in my collection only one cast and a few photographs and sketches. I have not yet been able to obtain a photograph of a series of prints, in order to study the walking picture. Nevertheless, we cannot simply ignore those footprints because we have a less than complete file of evidence concerning them. It is a fact that a many of all prints found in conjunction with ape-man sightings east of the Mississippi are of the 3-toed type.

Once again we are faced with a simple, if troublesome decision. Do we assume that all of the policemen, farmers, hunters, investigators and all the other good solid citizens who report such things are either fools or liars, or do we take the matter seriously?

If we take it seriously, we immediately come to a realization that we are dealing with a situation, in some ways, quite unlike anything we have heretofore encountered. There are elements involved here that are totally unique. No known primate normally has a foot with only three toes.

For that matter, I know of no mammal with three toes either. It is true that some creatures with five toes leave what appear to be 4-toed prints—members of the canine family being an example. But these 3-toed ape-man prints are obviously just that; the impressions left by feet with only three toes.

The 3-toed foot is very different from that of the Bigfoot/Sasquatch in several important ways in addition to the toe situation. Most notable is the different heel shape. In the majority of the 3-toed tracks, the foot shows a definite taper toward the heel, which is sometimes quite narrow. The Sasquatch heel, you will remember, is quite broad in proportion to the over-all size of the foot. Three-toed, swim-fin-shaped feet seem a most unlikely form of pedal equipment for a 7-foot-tall, massively proportioned, upright-walking creature. That, unfortunately, does not, in any way, eliminate the fact that there are obviously creatures of that description wandering around various localities of North America.

With fewer reports and very few researchers working on the reports from the areas east of the Mississippi, we have not, until recently, been able to acquire a file of detailed descriptions of the 3-toed giants. The excellent work of Stan Gordon's group in Pennsylvania in 1973 has created a change in that situation.

Time and time again in the Pennsylvania reports, we find particulars of physical description that are unknown to reports from the Northwest. The most outstanding feature of the Pennsylvania creatures is the large, bright red or orange, glowing eyes. While Bigfoot reports frequently mention eyes that reflect light, the Pennsylvania creatures' eyes were commonly reported as glowing, even in total darkness. Also, the eyes are apparently larger than those of the Bigfoot, several times described as large as golf balls.

Ears are almost never mentioned in Northwest reports, yet they were described in the majority of Pennsylvania incidents.

Prominent fangs, or "canine teeth," are rarely

mentioned in the Northwest reports, but were mentioned in nearly every close encounter with the Pennsylvania beasts. The arms of the Sasquatch appear to be slightly longer in proportion to torso length than is normal for man. However, the Pennsylvania monsters reportedly exhibit extreme arm length, in some cases the hands very nearly touch the ground.

As in the Bigfoot/Sasquatch reports, a most unpleasant stench was frequently reported, but in the case of the Pennsylvania creatures it was commonly described as a "chemical-type odor" or "a sulphur-like smell."

Sounds made by the creatures were most often described as either a piercing scream as if a man were in great pain, or a sound like that of a crying baby.

The behavior of the Pennsylvania creatures is notably different than that described in the majority of Northwest reports. The 3-toed monsters are much more likely to be observed in built-up areas than is the Bigfoot. Incredibly, the majority of the Pennsylvania sightings occurred in residential areas!

The Pennsylvania monsters are commonly reported approaching occupied homes and vehicles, where they peer in windows at the occupants. In a number of instances, the creatures closely approached humans, apparently out of curiosity. As indicated in the previous chapter, such behavior is not unknown in Northwest incidents, but is rare. In the case of the Eastern and Southern reports, it is extremely common behavior.

The UFO Connection

Perhaps most remarkable of all the circumstances surrounding the 3-toed monsters is the apparent UFO connection. Of course, even to give this particular matter any consideration at all, the reader must first accept the idea that our planet is being visited from time to time by beings from somewhere else in the universe. I have no comment to make on that subject except where the man-monsters seem to be involved. The following facts just cannot be ignored.

(A) In recent years, certain areas of North America have suddenly experienced a great deal of ape-man activity. In many cases, those areas had no historical background of such reports.

(B) Those same localities reported an unusual amount of UFO activity during the same period of time. Many readers are perhaps unaware that UFO sightings are still extremely common over the United States, even though they are less frequently reported in the press.

(C) Many witnesses—people of good reputation and well-respected in their communities—have reported seeing the creatures near where UFOs have landed and in some cases claimed to have seen them enter or leave the craft.

I am certainly not qualified to advance any theories to explain the apparent link between the UFOs and the ape-men. However, Hayden C. Hewes, director of the International Flying Object Bureau, believes they are possibly being used to collect plant and animal samples. A number of UFO researchers are of the opinion that the giants are controlled in some way, possibly by high-frequency radio signals. It has been suggested by some that those high-frequency signals might be the explanation for the weird behavior of domestic animals approached by the man-monsters. Dogs whine and exhibit great fear, cattle stampede, and horses become unmanageable.

In considering the possibility that these may be extra-terrestrial creatures, we can consider once again those 3-toed tracks. Typical Bigfoot tracks can, without any great imagination, be attributed to no more than a modern-day Gigantopithecus. The footprints, although quite different in some details from those of modern man, are actually quite similar to footprints of our pre-human ancestors. But where, in all the history of evolution, do we find a 3-toed foot among the primates? Despite the many un-answered questions relative to Bigfoot, that matter is like an open book in comparison to the 3-toed ape-man situation. Why do the creatures make their appearance in a certain area for a few months and then disappear. If it is no more than a migratory pattern, from whence do they come? What is their destination?

To create even more confusion, we must face the fact that while most reports of the 3-toed tracks are recent, some are not by any means. The Fouke Monster is an example.   Hairy, man-monsters that leave 3-toed footprints in the mud have been reported near Fouke, Arkansas, for many years. Unlike most other areas reporting the 3-toed creatures, the Fouke Monster or monsters make their appearance year after year. The latest report from that locality came to our attention in 1974. The Hope Arkansas Star reported that Bobby Ford and three other men chased a 6-foot man-animal into a nearby wooded area. It later returned to the house and grabbed Ford, but he escaped.

In recent years, we have received a steady flow of reports of the Skunk Ape of the extreme Southeastern U.S. Typical is the case that occurred near Brooksville, Florida, November 30, 1966. A girl, changing a tire on a lonely road, smelled an unpleasant odor. She looked up to see a tall creature with a pointed head and a face like an ape. It watched her with "big staring eyes" while she completed her task.

Northeastern Missouri became the center of ape-man activity during the summer of 1972. A number of citizens in and around the town of Louisiana, Missouri, reported a 7- or 8-foot, foul-smelling, man-monster who left 3-toed tracks.

That particular part of Missouri is just downriver from Murphysboro, Illinois, where considerable ape-man (and UFO) activity was reported in the spring of 1973.

Starting in the spring of 1973 and continuing to date, the Antelope Valley, 60 miles north of Los Angeles, has been the scene of regular 3-toed ape-man activity. As described in an earlier chapter, the most amazing thing about that particular area is the distinct possibility that at least two, and possibly three, types of ape-men seem to show up in that high desert region at one time or another. To my knowledge that is the only case in which more than one type of giant has been reported from the same locality.

Some other aspects of the Antelope Valley sightings are somewhat unusual. The only case in which eye coloring was mentioned was a sighting by the air police at Edwards Air Base at the north end of the valley. The eyes in that instance were described as bright blue, while practically all other reports connected with the 3-toed creatures mention orange or red-orange eyes.

Summary of Evidence

"Mo-Mo, the Missouri Monster," the "Skunk Ape," the "Fouke Monster," the "Pennsylvania Ape-man," the "Abominable Sandman," and the "Little Red Men of the Delta," are incredible names given to some theoretically "impossible" creatures. Nevertheless, a great many good citizens of this country, people from all walks of life and all sorts of backgrounds are convinced they have seen the man-monsters. Footprints of the 3- and 4-toed types have been cast and photographed. Hair and fecal specimens of the 3-toed creatures have been analyzed in professional laboratories. Newspaper reports from years past tell of shootings of the 4-toed desert creatures. A lengthy historical record exists concerning the dwarf ape-men. If nothing else, it seems there is considerable justification for massive research in this fascinating field. I will predict, however, based on the record, that no scientific research will take place. It is simply more convenient to believe that we know all we need to know about the inhabitants of the forests, deserts, and bayous of our continent. In the following chapter, I will attempt to draw some reasonable conclusions from the great mass of information we have collected relative to the man-monsters of North America.

Chapter 8
Some Monstrous Conclusions

At this point it seems logical to sum up the evidence and attempt to create a degree of order out of the confusing mass of information available. In so doing, we must repeat certain parts of the story.

The more than 1,000 reports in our files, even though backed up, in many cases, with photos and plaster casts of footprints, may not prove anything, but certain logical conclusions can be drawn from that evidence. It does require, however, that we retain a reasonably open mind.

Certain points are provable. It is a fact that a lot of two-legged, hairy "somethings" have been frightening the very devil out of people all over North America for a long time. Not only that, those same creatures are leaving some mighty funny-looking footprints in the soil and snow of our continent. So, let's try at this time to determine from the evidence, just what those things really are and where they have come from.

The information contained in early chapters makes evident the probability that there are several different types of man-monsters roaming this continent. The record is not yet clear as to how many different types there are or just how "different" they may be. I personally believe there are at least four distinct races and very possibly even more.

The best known of the four and the only one we really know anything about is the giant of the Northwest known as Bigfoot or Sasquatch. I have most frequently referred to them as creatures of the Northwest, although there is some evidence that they, can be found in most forested areas of North America. At this time, we can define their range as, roughly, all of Western Canada, the Western U.S. from Central California north and east at least as far as Michigan. These creatures are probably direct descendants of *Gigantopithecus*, and enormous Asian sub-humonid, supposedly long extinct. They doubtless arrived in North America the same way the Indians did—over a land bridge from Siberia. The Bigfoot/Sasquatch are the true giants among North American ape-men. The adult males range in height from 7- to 10-feet and the larger individuals probably weigh in excess of 1,000 pounds.

The arms are slightly longer and the legs a little shorter in relation to the torso, than in man. The head is large, the forehead slopes to a peak or crest and the neck is extremely short. The teeth are of more or less uniform size. The ears are not ordinarily visible. The hands are short and broad and the fingers are carried in a curved or scooped position.   Hair color varies, but is most commonly dark brown or black. Albinism may be fairly common with a surprising number of white individuals reported. In those reports, we usually also find red, reflective eye color noted. They are primarily nocturnal and or crepuscular in habits and are omnivorous. They appear to be non-territorial; their movements from one area to another are most-likely based upon availability of specific food products. They appear to travel in family groups, at least during part of the year. They appear to generally avoid close contact with man, especially when traveling in family groups. Lone males appear to be much bolder then the females or the young and are the ones who most commonly come into contact with man. They appear to be less active in the winter, although they may not hibernate in the true sense of the word.

They probably have no fire and no tools. They build no shelters, but possibly weave beds of pine and fir boughs.

They have no true speech, but are apparently able to communicate through various types of chattering, whistles and screams. A high-pitched, whistling scream is the sound most often reported. Their feet are short, broad, and lacking an arch. The heel is broad. The five toes are long and flexible, with a pad or webbing covering the first joint of the toes.   The Desert Ape-Man, called by some, the "Abominable Sandman" is apparently a somewhat smaller, but more aggressive creature. Judging by foot-shape alone, they cannot be considered merely a desert version of the Bigfoot. The strange "V"-shaped foot shows only four toes and its heel shape is entirely different than that of the Bigfoot/Sasquatch.

The range of these creatures is even less clearly understood. Most of the reports appear to center around the deserts and nearby mountains of extreme Southern California. The Dwarf Ape-Men or "mini-monsters," appear to be more man-like than any of the giants. Some of the more detailed descriptions from South America and Asia are surprisingly similar to information obtained from North American sightings.

They are apparently very shy, primarily nocturnal and to some degree arboreal. The most commonly-reported coloring is reddish-brown. The footprints exhibit a narrow heel and toes that were quite evenly aligned and of more-or-less uniform size.

Their range probably includes vast areas of river bottom along the Mississippi waterway and its tributaries. They probably inhabit many swamps and bayous of the southeastern United States and perhaps a few mountainous areas in Idaho and Montana. There are almost certainly some representatives of the species in a few remote mountainous regions of the far West.

The 3-toed Ape-Men appear to represent a problem unrelated to the three types mentioned above. Because of the apparent UFO involvement with these creatures I am going to go out on a very long, skinny limb and make the following prediction: When we eventually learn the truth about these 3-toed monster-men, we will find that they are trained or "programmed" specimens from another planet. I believe the evidence indicates they are brought here by and controlled by, intelligent beings who are cavorting about our planet in disc-shaped aircraft.

Perhaps earlier experiences in making contact with our planet convinced the space travelers that we are a bit too hostile for safety's sake and to avoid direct confrontation. So they use expendable animals to do their research. As preposterous a thought as that might be, let's keep in mind that we use monkeys for medical experiments so as not to endanger humans. Perhaps someone will eventually produce some evidence that will allow a better explanation relative to the 3-toed Ape-Men. In the meantime, we can only operate on the information at our disposal and that information clearly links the 3-toed creatures to UFOs.

These "alien" creatures exhibit certain characteristics that differentiate them from the other ape-man types.

The pedal structure is obviously unlike that of any known primate. The 3-toed, swim fin-shaped feet are so unlike any other feet on this planet, it would be difficult to convince ourselves that they belong here, even without the UFO-related information. The eyes, too, are unique. Rather than merely reflecting light, many witnesses state the eyes glow, even in total darkness.

These creatures also exhibit characteristics of physical structure that definitely differentiates them from the other ape-men. Their arms are longer, their heads are smaller, the ears are clearly visible and they have protuberant fangs.

Although considerably larger than man, they are not quite so enormous as the Sasquatch. They average about 7-feet in height and are not so massively proportioned as the Northwest giants.

The most common form of sound reported in relation to the 3-toed creatures is that of a crying baby. They also appear to attempt to mimic the sounds of man. Of the various ape-man types, these are the only ones that appear to habitually approach man. They give every evidence of great curiosity concerning man, often approaching homes or vehicles. They have repeatedly shown great interest in children or in homes containing children.

Are They Dangerous To Man?

We have, I think, established a pretty good case to justify our claim that several types of ape-men inhabit our continent. Those who examine the evidence and reach the same conclusion invariably ask the same question, "Are they dangerous to man?" I think the best over-all answer to that question is that, like any large, wild creature, they are capable of harming man, but prefer to avoid conflict whenever possible.

This is really a very important matter, if for no other reason than the fact that since we are now becoming aware that we share the continent with ape-men, we should be prepared to deal with them intelligently. Every year, throughout North America, hundreds of thousands of people go into the forests for work or play. Are they in any real danger from the man-monsters, and if so, how can they best avoid conflict with them?

The most encouraging point in this discussion is the very fact that so many hunters, fishermen, timber cruisers, hikers, campers and others do go into the forests each year and return unscathed. There appears to be one or more types of ape-man in nearly every state, but we have very few incidents on record of attacks by them.

Even the various Indian tribes disagreed as to the ferocity of the creatures, although the consensus of opinion seemed to be that they were best left alone. Some tribes insisted that the ape-men were man-eaters and there are also a number of tribal tales of kidnappings by the ape-men. In most cases, the victims were women or children.

Because we appear to be dealing with several distinct types of man-monsters, perhaps it would be advisable to discuss the matter of possible danger to man, in relation to each type.

Because of its great size, we can assume that the Sasquatch is potentially very dangerous. However, judging by the hundreds of face-to-face encounters between Bigfoot and Man, it appears that the giants do, in the vast majority of cases, indicate a strong desire to avoid contact. However, we must also keep in mind the fact that all creatures, wild or domestic, are individuals. There is always the possibility of one or more of the ape-men reacting to Man in a manner that is quite unlike what others of the species have done. The same, 7-foot, 600 or 700 pound female that fled from Patterson and Gimlin in Bluff Creek, might well have turned on them and killed them both had she been accompanied by her young. Any one of the giants is capable of committing quick and total mayhem upon the relatively fragile body of a mere human.

We do, in fact, have some reports of encounters with the Sasquatch in which the giants acted in an aggressive, if not really dangerous, manner.

John Green interviewed a Wilsonville, Oregon, woman who described being thrown over a fence by a Sasquatch.

Just as she climbed through a barbed-wire fence at the edge of a field on her farm, something grabbed her and threw her about 15 feet. She stated that the creature had course dark hair on its arms and huge, human-like hands, with no hair on the palms.

The woman's husband heard her screams and arrived in time to help her from the thistle bush in which she had landed, but did not see the giant. A strong, musky odor was noted on the woman's clothes. The odor lasted for several hours.

It does appear that the giants have great fear of

firearms and invariably flee when shot or shot at. In fact, to sum up this question of possible Sasquatch ferocity, we can point to the record. We do not have a single case in our files in which a human has been killed or seriously injured in an unprovoked attack by one of the giants.

The mysterious 4-toed monsters of the Southwest deserts may be another matter, entirely. There is no proof that the gruesome events of Dead Man's Hole were the work of an ape-man, but the circumstances involved make it appear likely. Reports from the deserts and mountains of the Southwest demonstrate a possibly hostile attitude on the part of the giants from that area.

On November 8, 1958, Charles Wetzel of Bloomington, California, reported to the police that his vehicle had been attacked by a strange creature near Riverside. He stated that while driving home, late at night, a giant, shaggy creature with a round face and shiny eyes leapt in front of his car and scratched at the windshield with long arms.

On August 26, a teenager, Jerri Mendenhall, reported to the sheriff's department that she and some other teenagers had encountered an ape-man near Fontana, California. According to the press report, she claimed that as they were driving along a lonely dirt road just north of town, a 7-foot tall, hairy man stepped out of the bushes and grabbed at her through a car window.

Several years after the incident I had the opportunity to question the witness as to the details of the incident. I felt that, despite the passage of time, she might be able to supply details heretofore overlooked. I also felt that if the case was a hoax, as the sheriff's department suggested, the witness, now grown and married, might be willing to admit that it was all just a teenage prank. When I did interview her, she appeared quite surprised that anyone was still interested in the incident. Interestingly, her husband did not even know she had been involved, although he remembered a number of other teenagers talking about having seen the ape-man in the Lover's Lane area, behind the Fontana Raceway.

The witness, now Mrs. Oberlis, stated that the incident was, indeed, very real. She and her girl friend, accompanied by a young nephew, drove into the area in an effort to see the ape-man that had been reported by other teenagers. As she was backing slowly down a narrow road, the giant stepped out of the bushes and grabbed for her, scratching her face and neck. She screamed, jammed the accelerator down and backed out of the area, as the creature walked off into the darkness.

Mrs. Oberlis emphasized one point that had not been mentioned by the press. The beast had a strong, unpleasant odor. I find that particularly significant because she apparently had no knowledge of the Bigfoot research that has produced so many reports of the giants and their odor.

The most tragic events that may be connected to the ape-men are the numerous disappearances of children in the San Gabriel Mountains near Los Angeles. On several occasions during my career with the Los Angeles Sheriff's Department, I was involved in investigation of cases in which children had disappeared in the foothills. In several of those cases, no trace has ever been found, despite the efforts of the nation's largest sheriff's department and some of the finest search and rescue organizations in the world.

Of course, there is no direct evidence linking those

disappearances to the ape-men, but the apparent hostile and aggressive nature of the 4-toed giants lead me to believe there may be some connection. For example, the reader will recall a reference to an all-night stakeout mentioned in Chapter 3. In that instance, working on information that ape-man evidence had been found in a certain canyon north of Pasadena, a group of researchers spent a frightening night on stakeout. They were bombarded with boulders, larger than a man could lift and repeatedly heard deep, bellowing roars echoing through the canyon. The mouth of that same canyon was the scene of one of the above-mentioned disappearances, some years ago. Despite the stories told by the Indians, we have only one case in our files in which one of the Dwarf Ape-Men approached a human being. In that case, the attacker, if that is what he was, was easily driven off when struck with a rifle barrel.

Actually, with so few incidents involving the dwarfs, we have little on which to base any conclusions regarding their possible danger to man. There are a number of Southern folks who frighten their children with stories of the fierce "Woolyboogers," but whether or not the stories are based on fact, is unknown.

In any case, their small size would seem to be sufficient reason to deter them from attacking humans, or at least adult humans.

Despite the fact that the 3-toed creatures are more frequently found near human habitation than the other types, there is only one case indicating a direct attack. Because the man was not injured in that case, it seems doubtful that the creature intended great harm.

The 3-toed Ape-Men have been shot at and shot, struck by cars, pursued by police dogs and otherwise harassed, but they appear to be unwilling to attack humans.

So, are the ape-men of North America dangerous to man? With the possible exception of the strange 4-toed giants of the Southern California deserts, the answer is apparently, no they are not. At least, no more dangerous than any other wild beast that tries to avoid man and has lots of rugged territory in which to elude him.

Future Research

I feel that we already know about all we are likely to learn concerning the Northwest giants until science has had an opportunity to examine one in the flesh. In the meantime, there is a great need for further study of the dwarfs and the desert giants. I for one, am going to leave the matter of the 3-Toed Ape-Men to the UFOlogists, but there is certainly room for considerably more study in that area.

All in all, the situation regarding research remains much the same as it has been all along. Despite some grandiose statements by certain Bigfoot investigators, the bulk of the research is still being carried on by amateurs working more or less independently.

The Bigfoot Dilemma

In the few remaining paragraphs, I will once again be limiting my comments to those ape-men apparently indigenous to our planet. Because the 3-toed giants are apparently a different problem altogether, I will do as an anthropologist might do and simply ignore those problems that don't fit neatly into our puzzle.

In discussing the best methods of bringing an ape-man in, dead or alive, we must ask ourselves, first, if we have the right to do so. If these creatures are to be simply considered as animals, then perhaps our responsibility is no greater than it would be in the case of any other rare beast. But is Bigfoot a mere beast or is he a man, or perhaps neither? I have heard this point argued among Bigfoot researchers time and again. As some point out, either a creature is a man or it is not. The ape-men appear to have no true speech, no fire, no clothes, no tools and they are covered with hair, so should they be considered in a class with the gorillas and other primates below man?

Some Australian aborigines still live without even the crudest of shelters, without clothes and with only the most simple tools and weapons. Their vocabulary is extremely limited and they have sloping foreheads and heavy brow ridges. Yet they are considered to be the species, *Homo Sapiens*.

Bigfoot walks upright as does no "known" primate but man.

Most anthropologists believe that man proceeded from "ape or proto-man to man," when he began to walk upright, freeing his hands to make and use simple tools. We have no proof that Bigfoot does not use small stone or wooden tools for digging and grubbing for food.

The matter of hairiness is hardly a deciding factor in this discussion. Some anthropologists feel that the branch of ape-men who became true men lost their hair when conditions forced them to leave the forests and live in the savannas and deserts. He was then forced to give up his vegetarian habits and become a hunter, running down and killing small animals. For such purposes a heavy coating of insulating fur would have been a hindrance, so the hair was lost. Could it not be that other, similar creatures remained in the forests, retaining their hair covering?

This discussion may appear to be purely academic, but is it'? The fact is that one of these days, (possibly as this is being written), someone will kill a man-monster and bring it to science. What have we then, a case of murder, or just an interesting zoological oddity? Some court somewhere, is going to have to make a decision.

Not only the courts, but other governmental agencies, will face some most unique problems when this happens. When protective laws are passed, are they to be mere game laws like any other statutes protecting rare animals, or are they to be added to our penal code? Is it possible that murder and manslaughter sections of our penal codes already apply?

If the courts decide that the giants are truly man-like beings, it might seem a bit facetious to suggest that they should then have all the rights and privileges as other humans; or is it?

If naturalists and public opinion demand that Bigfoot's habitat be set aside as protective areas, what will be the reaction of the lumber and other industries that depend upon those forests for their survival? To properly protect the giants, it might be necessary to set aside vast areas of mountainous forests and leave them in a true wilderness state, "unimproved" by man.

Even if such lands are not closed off entirely, there remains the question as to how many hunters, fishermen, campers and others are going to be willing to venture into those forests once it becomes common knowledge than 9-foot hairy giants are inhabitants therein.

Science will most surely want some specimens for study, but again, do we have that right? If it is decided that they are man-creatures then anyone who captures and carries a Bigfoot off to the zoo, will most likely have committed kidnapping.

Even though the giants look like oversize men covered in hair, we might make an exception and call them "not quite men." In that case, we might just say that they do not qualify for the rights and the protection of "real men." That, however, might be a dangerous precedent. What of the next tribe of really primitive natives that comes to the attention of anthropologists in New Guinea or South America? Will we make an exception in their case and cart a few off to zoos or museums?

The decisions reached by our courts and the legislation that is passed by our state and federal governments might very well determine whether or not the fascinating story of these amazing creatures will come to an abrupt end in our time. No matter what the legal considerations, do we have the moral right to bring to a close such an important chapter in the story of evolution?

Another interesting problem that will be created when the ape-man story becomes popular knowledge is the matter of religious belief. There are millions of people who, because of their religious principles, cannot accept the belief in evolution. What will their reaction be when science presents them with a living, breathing example of man's evolution?

These and many similar questions will have to be answered one of these days—perhaps soon. One thing is certain... There exist today, in some of the forests, deserts and bayous of North America several races or types of sub-human creatures. Call them what you will—Abominable Snowmen, ape-men, Sasquatch, *giantopithicus*, or Bigfoot. We can no longer ignore the evidence, because they are right here where they have been all the time.

So this is Bigfoot—Man's poor relation—who has come ambling down the halls of time into the 20th century... a living reminder of Man's dim and distant past.

About the Editors

Joe Blakely lives with his wife, Saundra Miles in Eugene, Oregon. He has one son, Justin, and a stepson, Jonathan Baker. Mr. Blakely earned a degree in history from San Diego State College—while in college he excelled in the writing of history term papers.

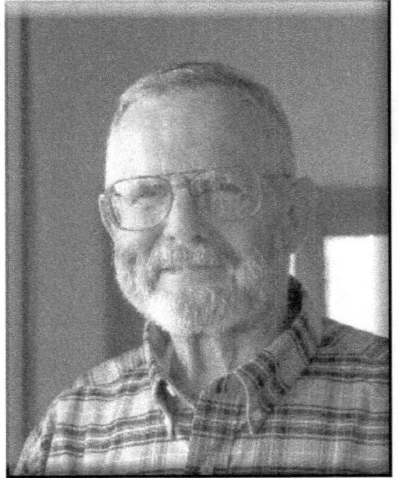

Mr. Blakely retired from the Office of Public Safety at the University of Oregon in 1999. After retirement he decided to write about Oregon history.

Mr. Blakely has written eleven books—eight are histories about Oregon. Mr. Blakely says his best work is his biography of Oswald West, Oregon's rascally governor who wrote legislation in 1913 to set aside Oregon's beaches as a highway, thereby providing public access. His two Highway 101 coast books, *Lifting Oregon Out of the Mud: Building the Oregon Coast Highway* (2006) and *Building Oregon's Coast Highway 1936-1966: Straightening Curves and Uncorking Bottlenecks* (2014) on building the coast highway, have been most popular.

Mr. Blakely is currently working on his fifth Bigfoot novel.

To contact Joe Blakely, you can write him at
PO Box 51561, Eugene, OR 97405
https://joeblakelyauthor.wordpress.com/

About the Editors

Pat Edwards is the author of two books on the history of her home community of Lorane, Oregon. The first, *Sawdust and Cider; A History of Lorane, Oregon and the Siuslaw Valley*, was written with co-authors Nancy O'Hearn and Marna Hing in 1987 to help celebrate the community's centennial. In 2006, Pat wrote a major revision of the book called *From Sawdust and Cider to Wine*.

She and her husband Jim own the Lorane Family Store and Pat spent 15 years as Administrative Coordinator for the Institute of Neuroscience at the University of Oregon.

Since her retirement from the UO, Pat has taken on the role of owner and managing editor of a small press publishing company, *Groundwaters* Publishing LLC, which distributed a literary quarterly magazine throughout all of Lane County, Oregon for over 10 years of publication. She and her colleague, Jennifer Chambers, are now publishing it as an annual anthology.

In 2014, Pat and her co-author, Jo-Brew, completed over 3 years of joint research and compilation of two volumes on the history of the Pacific Highway/U.S.

Highway 99 through Oregon called *OREGON'S MAIN STREET: U.S. Highway 99; "The Stories"* and *"The Folk History."* They toured throughout Oregon, giving talks to historical societies, libraries and service clubs on the history of the highway until Jo's death on March 1, 2018.

Pat has also begun writing a series of books on early Lane County, Oregon settlers who had connections to Lorane, Oregon. The first is titled *The Baileys of Bailey Hill* (2017), followed by *The Life and Letters of Captain John O'Brien* (2018). She is currently working on the third book of the series which highlights three families who were part of the Lost Wagon Train of 1853.

Pat writes a weekly column for two local Lane County weeklies, the *Fern Ridge Review* of Veneta and the *Creswell Chronicle* of Creswell, Oregon.

In 2019, she and Jim will have been married for 55 years and they have five adult children, eleven grandchildren, and seven great-grands.

To contact Pat Edwards, you can write her at

PO Box 50, Lorane, OR 97451 or
edwards@groundwaterspublishing.com
https://allthingslorane.com or
http://groundwaterspublishing.com

Groundwaters Publishing, LLC
P.O. Box 50
Lorane, OR 97451
http://groundwaterspublishing.com

www.ingramcontent.com/pod-product-compliance
Lightning Source LLC
Chambersburg PA
CBHW060325030426
42336CB00011B/1211